ABOUT CANADA

Earle Gray

ISBN 978-1-895589-95-5
About Canada.

Published by Civil Sector Press
Box 86, Station C
Toronto, Ontario M61 3M7 Canada
Telephone: 416-345-9403.
Fax: 416-345-9403

Library and Archives Canada Cataloguing in Publication.

Gray, Earle, 1931. About Canada : "My God, this is a great country" / Earle Gray.

Includes index. ISBN 978-1-895589-95-5

1. Canada—History—Anecdotes.° I. Title.

FC176.G73 2012   971   C2012-906493-9

Author's books

CONTENTS

This modest book is dedicated
to all Canadians—white, black, brown,
Christians, Buddhist, atheists, all creeds and
races— who make Canada the most diverse,
peaceful, harmonious, and best country in the
world in which to live.

ACKNOWLEDGEMENTS
I am gratefully indebted to writer Munro Scott and historians Desmond Morton and
Robert Bothwell, for helpful comments and suggestions. Professor Morton challenged
me to challenge the popular view of history that Canada's destiny was forged by General
Wolfe on the Plains of Abraham. I did. The result is Chapter 5, without which this book
would have been bereft of a crucial, and little appreciated aspect of one of the most
important episodes of Canadian history. I'm indebted as well to the keen historical
insight of Professor Bothwell.

CHAPTER ONE
The things they say

My God, this is a great country

Wonderful are the things that have been said about Canada. Also contemptuous, insulting, praising, wise, witty, hopeful and hopeless things. Things said by Canadians, and by those who help us "see ourselves as others see us."

MY GOD, this is a great country. I chose this country, it didn't choose me. That means I am Canadian first, then Chinese... when you choose a new country, it should come first. *Wanda Clute (1958-),a native of China, on celebrating her first 20 years in Canada after overcoming initial obstacles and difficult adjustments in a new land. Interview,* Toronto Star, *January 24, 1999.*

"YOU MUST COME TO CANADA. This is a wonderful place. I'm in jail and eat meat three times a day," he tells his St. Petersburg friend. There was a long pause, and then the man in St. Petersburg asked in a surprised voice, "Meat?" Canadian convict: "Yes, three times a day." Another pause, and then the other man, sounding almost awed, asks: "Meat and potatoes?" Canadian convict:

"Yes. You should come here and commit a crime." *Overheard telephone conversation by a Russian gangster serving time in a Canadian jail for petty crime, speaking to a friend in Russia. John Duncanson and Philip Mascoll in "Russian mob crime soars in Canada,"* Toronto Star, *June 22, 1996.*

WORLD'S BEST. Canada is today the most successful pluralist society on the face of the globe, without any doubt in my mind... That is something unique to Canada. It is an amazing global asset. *Aga Khan IV (1936-), spiritual leader of Ismaili Muslims.* Toronto Globe and Mail, *February 2, 2002.*

WORLD IMAGE. There is probably no country in the world that reflects the population of the planet more fully than does Canada. Links of family, emotion, culture, religion and ideology exist between millions of Canadians and societies abroad. *Ward Elcock, director of the Canadian Security Intelligence Service, in remarks at Senate committee hearings.* Toronto Star, *October 30, 1998.*

AS FOR OUR DIVERSITY, it is a tremendous asset. New Canadians who come here seeking opportunity have enriched our knowledge through their customs, cultures, contacts, and markets... Managing our contrasts and embracing our diversity leads to tremendous advantages for Canadian companies as they expand worldwide. *Timothy Reid, president, Canadian Chamber of Commerce.* Canadian Speeches, *January 1998.*

DIVERSE FEDERATION. In our own federation we [will] have Catholic and Protestant, English, French, Irish and Scotch, and each by his efforts and his success [will] increase the prosperity and glory of the new Confederacy...[We are] of different races, not for the purpose of warring against each other, but in order to compete and emulate for the general welfare. *George-Etienne Carter (1814-73), speech, Canada Legislative Assembly, Quebec, February 7, 1865.*

WHAT SETS CANADIAN SOCIETY apart from others is that ours is an inclusive society... Canadian citizenship recognizes differences. It praises diversity. It is what we as Canadians choose to have in common with each other. It is a bridge between those who left somewhere to make a new home and those born here. What keeps the bridge strong is tolerance, fairness and compassion. *Denise Chong, author of* The Concubine's Daughter, *a finalist for the 1994 Governor General's Literary Awards, lecture, "Being Canadian."* Canadian Speeches, *May 1995.*

TOO MUCH MEMORY. Canadians, like their historians, have spent too much time remembering conflicts, crises, and failures. They forgot the great, quiet continuity of life in a vast and generous land. A cautious people learns from its past; a sensible people can face its future. Canadians, on the whole, are both. *Desmond Morton (1937-), historian.* A Short History of Canada *(2006).*

BLESS THE GOOD PEOPLE of Halifax who did not sleep, who took strangers into their homes, who opened their hearts and shelters, who rushed in enough food and clothing to supply an army, who offered tours of their beautiful city and, above all, who listened with a simple empathy that brought this tough and fully grown man to tears, over and over again. I heard not a single harsh word, saw not the slightest gesture of frustration, and felt nothing but pure and honest welcome... we will always share this bond of your unstinting hospitality to people who descended upon you as frightened strangers, and received nothing but solace and solidarity in your embrace of goodness.

Stephen Jay Gould (1941-2002), U.S. paleontologist and author, was one of more than 25,000 U.S. passengers stranded at Canadian airports when U.S.-bound aircraft were diverted because of the September 11, 2001 terrorist attacks on the World Trade Centre in New York and on Washington. "Ode to human decency: bless the good people of Halifax," Toronto Globe and Mail, *September 20, 2001.*

CANADIAN PARADOX. Twenty-five years of public opinion polling in Canada have taught me a seemingly paradoxical truth: Canadians feel strongly about their weak attachment to Canada, its political institutions, and their fellow citizens. *Michael Adams. President of Environics Research Group Ltd.* Sex In The Snow: Canadian Social Values At The End of The Millennium. *Toronto (1997).*

CANADA HAS SHOWN the world how to balance freedom with compassion and tradition with innovation, in your efforts to provide health care to all your citizens, to treat your senior citizens with the dignity and respect they deserve, to take on tough issues like the move afoot to outlaw automatic weapons designed for killing and not for hunting. *Bill Clinton, 42nd U.S. president. Address to a joint session of Parliament, 1995.*

DEAD CANADA. There is no galvanizing a corpse! Canada is dead—dead church, dead commerce, dead people. A poor, priest-ridden, politician-ridden, doctor-ridden, lawyer-ridden land. No energy, no enterprise, no snap. *Toronto* Leader, *April 28, 1870.*

CANADA IS FINISHED. It simply cannot make it because of its taxation and left-wing politics. It can change but it will be too painful. *Victor Rice, chairman of Varity Corp., an auto parts maker, on moving its head office from Toronto to Buffalo.* Financial Post, *Toronto, October 27, 1994.*

CANADA HAS AVAILABLE to her the best of everything—British politics, French culture, American technology. Unfortunately she settles for French politics, American culture and British technology. *Anonymous.* Financial Post, *May 2, 1964.*

EVEN MORE PRECIOUS than life is my native Canada. She is a funny country to love with her frozen north, her rocky barren tracks, her mountains and her lakes. She is always toddling along behind her neighbour to the south. I would love Canada if there were no people—sometimes I feel I would prefer it. *Frederick Banting (1891-1941), Canadian physiologist, co-discoverer, with Charles H. Best, of insulin. Quoted by Michael Bliss in* Canadian Business magazine, *December 1992.*

Canadians feel strongly about their weak attachment to Canada.

FIT FOR QUARRELS. I wish the British Government would give you Canada at once. It is fit for nothing but to breed quarrels. *Alexander Baring (1774-1848), English banker and diplomat. Letter to John Quincy Adams, U.S. Ambassador, London, 1816.*

ESCAPE. Get over the border as soon as you can; come to London or go to New York; shake the dust of Canada from your feet. Get out of a land that is willing to pay money for whisky, but wants its literature free in the shape of Ayer's Almanac. *Robert Barr (1850-1920), Canadian novelist. Canadian Magazine, November 1899.*

SQUARE. Canada is a country so square that even the female impersonators are women. *Richard Benner (1936-), screenwriter.* Outrageous *(film, 1977).*

WE SEEK SOVEREIGNTY because it is absolutely essential. It is a necessity for Quebec, like the ripening of a fruit, like reaching adulthood, like the conclusions of a logical argument, like the discovery which crowns a voyage of exploration, like the opening of a river into the ocean. *Lucien Bouchard (1938-), Quebec politician, leader of the Bloc Quebecois, later premier of Quebec. Speech, Montreal, April 7, 1995. "Quick turn in Quebec's march to independence," Canadian Speeches, May 1995.*

AMERICAN CANADIANS. Americans you already are by your language, your nasal accent, your common slang, your dress, your daily habits; by the Yankee literature with which your homes and clubs are flooded; by your yellow journals and their rantings; by your loud and intolerant patriotism; by your worship of gold, snobbery and titles. *Henri Bourassa (1868-1951), Quebec politician, journalist, and newspaper publisher.* The Spectre of Annexation and the Real Danger of National Disruption *(1912).*

FAVOURITE SONS. You call your leaders favourite sons. We go all the way and say what they're sons of. *Dave Broadfoot (1925-), Canadian actor, humourist and writer, on the difference between Canadians and Americans.* Toronto Star, *July 16, 2001.*

COLOUR YOUR LIFE. I sometimes wonder if the Canadian liking for bright colours isn't the outcome of that prolonged session of white during the winter months. *Lady (Evelyn) Byng (1870-1949, wife of Viscount Byng, governor general of Canada, 1921-26.* Up the Stream of Time *(1945).*

EMIGRATION. It was computed, after careful examination, that by 1896 at least every third able-bodied man in Canada between the ages of 20 and 40 had emigrated to the United States. *Richard Cartwright (1835-1912), Canadian statesman and free trade advocate.* Reminiscences *(1912).*

LINCHPIN. Canada is the linchpin of the English-speaking world. Canada, with those relations of friendly, affectionate intimacy with the United States on the one hand and with her unswerving fidelity to the British Commonwealth and the Motherland on the other, is the link which joins together these great branches of the human family, a link which, spanning the oceans, brings the continents into their true relation. *Winston Churchill (1874-1965). Speech, London, England, September 4, 1941.*

TOSSED SALAD. Canada has never been a melting pot, more like a tossed salad. *Arnold Edinborough (1922-2006), Canadian writer and arts critic.* Canada and The World, *Toronto, April 1994.*

LOCAL FOREIGNERS. I meet English Canadians. For me, they are like Greeks or Turks. I am curious to get to know them as individuals, but I don't belong to the same nation. *Christian Gagnon, Quebec separatist politician, speaking as a Bloc Quebecois* *candidate for election to Parliament.* Vancouver Sun, *September 25, 1993.*

PATRIOTISM. I was brought up in Southwestern Ontario where we were taught that Canadian patriotism should not withstand anything more than a five-dollar-a-month wage differential. Anything more than that and you went to Detroit. *John Kenneth Galbraith (1908-2006), Canadian-born Harvard University economist, author and diplomat. Cited by Theo Cheney in* Getting the Words Right *(2005).*

CANADA FROM SPACE. I have seen Canada from space. Its size and beauty left me breathless. We Canadians have received much, much more than our share. *Marc Garneau (1949-), first Canadian astronaut. Toronto* Globe and Mail, *July 17, 1997.*

You call your leaders favourite sons. We go all the way and say what they're sons of.

SOLUTION. Canada is the solution looking for a problem. *Augustin Gomez, former Mexican ambassador to Canada. Quoted by David Kilgour, MP, in a speech, October 14, 1994.*

ALCOHOLICS. We were rather surprised that in Ontario we had to register at the local liquor store as alcoholics. *Alec Guiness (1914-2000), British actor.* Blessings in Disguise *(1985).*

WOLVES are scarce in Canada, but they afford the finest furs in all the country. Their flesh is white, and good to eat; they pursue their prey to the tops of the tallest trees. *William Guthrie.* Guthrie's Geographic Grammar *(1807).*

FELLER CITIZENS, this country is goin' to the dogs hand over hand. *Thomas C. Haliburton (1796-1865), Canadian jurist and author, best known as the creator of Sam Slick, the Yankee clock peddler.* Sam Slick *(1853).*

THOSE FROZEN to death display on their visages a look of contentment achieved only by successful religious mystics. *William Hales Hingston (1829-1907), Canadian physician and politician.* The Climate of Canada and its Relation to Life and Health *(1884).*

NO ONE KNOWS my country, neither the stranger nor its own sons. My country is hidden in the dark and teeming brain of youth upon the eve of its manhood. My country has not found itself nor felt its power nor learned its true place. It is all visions and doubts and hopes and dreams. It is strength and weakness, despair and joy, and the wild confusions and restless strivings of a boy who has passed his manhood but is not yet a man. *Bruce Hutchison (1901-92), journalist and author.* The Unknown Country *(1942).*

AS THE FRIGID TUNDRA keeps Canada's population from spreading northward, America's loud materialism, unruly style and social problems keep Canadians from straying south. That hundred-mile-wide belt of population from the Atlantic to the Pacific has endured as a subtly distinctive community, one that many citizens want to preserve. English and French Canadians might not mind separating from each other, but immigrants from throughout the world may demand Canada's continued existence. For them, Canada provides unlimited freedom and economic opportunity while offering protection from the ruthless laissez-faire capitalism of the United States. *Robert D. Kaplan, U.S. journalist and author.* Atlantic Monthly, *August 1998.*

VICHYSSOISES. In any world menu, Canada must be considered the Vichyssoises of nations—it's cold, half French, and difficult to stir. *Stuart Keate (1913-87), Canadian newspaper publisher.* Maclean's, *August 8, 1994.*

The tragedy of this country is that French Canadians never forget history, and English Canadians never remember.

TOO MUCH. If some countries have too much history, we have too much geography. *William Lyon Mackenzie King (1874-1950), prime minister 1921-28; 1926-30; 1935-48. House of Commons, Debates, June 18, 1936.*

CURIOUS COUNTRY. Canada is perhaps the only country in the world held together by curiosity, the question being: can a nation, so structured and governed as Canada, endure? It would appear that through 115 years of often violent debate, no one is quite prepared to give up on her yet; as if we all have some lingering desire to see how this ongoing exercise in nation-building ends. *Ralph Klein (1942-), Canadian politician, Alberta premier. Speech, February 10, 1982.*

BRITISH PROTECTION. If you ask me as a French-Canadian why I am deeply attached to Great Britain, it is because I find in her institutions and under her flag all the protection I need. It is because she has been in the world the nurse of liberty. She has understood better than any other nation the art of government. *Rodolphe Lemieux (1866-1937), Canadian lawyer, Liberal politician and diplomat. Speech, Toronto, March 1905.*

SEPARATISTS. These overgrown children, these untrained do-it-yourselfers, these quacks who tamper with our political ideals, these peddlers of panaceas who, as dabblers, have discovered truths which escaped the knowledge of the laboratories. These people adore imitating the gestures of an adult, that is, all the gestures except one: paying the bill. *Jean Lesage (1912-80), Quebec politician, premier 1960-66, referring to Quebec separatists. Speech to Canadian Women's Press Club, Montreal, June 12, 1965. Translation. Quoted by Robert M. Hamilton and Dorothy Shields in The Dictionary of Canadian Quotations and Phrases (1982).*

MOOSE PEOPLE. Moose are just like some people—they are hard to train. *Shane*

Mahoney, chief wildlife researcher for the government of Newfoundland, on the difficulty in keeping moose from being attracted by the four million pounds of salt spread on Canadian highways every winter, resulting in dangerous moose-car collision, about 500 a year just in Newfoundland. Wall Street Journal, *January 16, 1995.*

MY LOVE FOR CANADA was a feeling nearly allied to that which the condemned criminal entertains for his cell—his only hope of escape being through the portals of the grave. *Susanna Moodie (1803-85), English-born Canadian writer and pioneer settler.* Roughing It In The Bush *(1852).*

NOT LIFE, LIBERTY, and the pursuit of happiness, but peace, order, and good government are what the national government of Canada guarantees. Under these, it is assumed, life, liberty, and happiness may be achieved, but by each according to his taste. For the society of allegiance admits of a diversity, the society of compact does not, and one of the blessings of Canadian life is that there is no Canadian way of life, much less two, but a unity under the Crown admitting of a thousand diversities. *W.L. Morton (1908-80), Canadian historian.* The Canadian Identity *(1961).*

HISTORY'S TRAGEDY. I sometimes think that the tragedy of this country is that French Canadians never forget history, and

We Canadians are standing on the mountain top of human wealth, freedom and privilege.

English Canadians never remember. *John Roberts (1933-2007), Canadian Liberal politician. Speech, Toronto, September 25, 1977.*

WE DON'T WANT to be paying 75 grand a year to knock on a door for a throne speech. Buy a doorbell.

Walter Robinson, director of the Canadian Taxpayer Federation, on the appointment of Mary McLaren as the first female "Gentleman Usher of the Black Rod," a position in the Canadian Senate that pays between $73,400 and $86,400 a year. In addition to administrative duties, the principal ceremonial function is to summon members of Parliament to the Senate chamber at the opening of Parliament by pounding on the House of Commons door with a black rod. The parliamentary tradition dates back to fourteenth-century England. Toronto Star, *October 21, 1997.*

NO AMERICAN who has chosen to leave the United States and take another citizenship will ever be a passionate nationalist anywhere, for what has turned us away from our own country is precisely that super-patriotism that has led to so many grievous mistakes both inside and outside the country. I will never be a super-Canadian, but in that I feel at home in a country which practices modesty and self-criticism regularly. *Jane Rule (1931-) U.S.-born Canadian writer. Toronto* Globe and Mail, *April 16, 1980.*

TO BE POOR in America means you are not trying very hard. To be poor in Canada means that the government is not trying hard enough. *Val Sears, Canadian journalist.* Toronto Star, *August 13, 1977.*

WHEN GREAT BRITAIN dismantled the British Empire it gave the land back to the original owners in Africa and Asia. This was not the case in Canada. *Noel Starblanket (1946-), Canadian Indian chief. Speech at a conference in London, July 6, 1979.*

KILLER COLD. I've played in some cold NFL cities like Green Bay and Buffalo and I hear it can get worse up in Canada. Any player ever die in the cold weather during a game up there? *Joe Toliver, U.S. quarterback on the possibility of playing in the Canadian Football League. Toronto* Globe and Mail, *March 15, 1995.*

WE PEER so suspiciously at each other that we cannot see that we Canadians are standing on the mountain top of human wealth, freedom and privilege. *Pierre Elliott Trudeau (1919-2000), fifteenth prime minister. Comment in 1980, cited in Toronto* Globe and Mail, *December 14, 1995.*

THE MAJORITY of Quebecers are not bilingual. Just like you, most of them speak only one language. There are about five million francophones in Quebec—and three-quarters of them speak only French.

Think of it: about as many Quebecers who speak only French as the combined total population of all three Prairie Provinces. *Pierre Trudeau, Speech, American Association of Broadcaster, Winnipeg, April 17, 1997.*

CANADA is not a country for the cold of heart or the cold of feet. *Pierre Trudeau, Toronto* Globe and Mail, *September 12, 1994.*

HOMELESS. Winters may be colder and longer in Toronto but the city's homeless suffer only half the death rate of the homeless in Boston, New York and Philadelphia, according to a study by St. Michael's Hospital Inner City Health Research Unit in Toronto. "People who are homeless in the U.S. tend not to have any medical insurance," says Dr. Stephen Whang, an American physician who has treated homeless patients in both Boston and Toronto. "But in Canada, even the poorest members of society have access to health care." The homeless in Toronto aged 35 to 54 are 58 percent less likely to die during a one-year period than those living on the streets of Philadelphia, 48 percent less likely than those in Boston, and 39 percent less likely than in New York. Homeless men in the United States 18-24 are five times more likely to be murdered than those in Canada." *Homeless less likely to die in Canada than U.S.," National Post, April 26, 2000.*

Manifest destiny, eh?

Manifest Destiny, the American doctrine that sought to absorb Canada within its borders, was a big factor in early Canadian-American history, the embers of which were still flickering at least as late as 2000.

TAKE QUEBEC. The unanimous Voice of the Continent is Canada must be ours; Quebec must be taken. *John Adams (1735-1826), second U.S. president, following the 1776 defeat of an invasion of Canada by U.S. armies led by Richard Montgomery and Benedict Arnold.*

AN INVITATION. Canada, acceding to this confederation, and joining in the measures of the United States, shall be admitted into, and entitled to all the advantages of this Union: but no other colony shall be admitted into the same unless such admission be agreed to by nine states. *U.S. Articles of Confederation, November 15, 1777.*

SEDUCTION. The people of that country [Canada] are first to be seduced from their allegiance, and converted into traitors, as preparatory to the making them good citizens. *John Randolph (1773-1833), U.S. politician and orator. U.S. Congress, December 10, 1811.*

A MATTER OF MARCHING. The annexation of Canada this year as far as the neighbourhood of Quebec, will be a mere matter of marching, and will give us experience for the attack of Halifax the next, and the final expulsion of England from the American continent. *Thomas Jefferson (1743-1826), third U.S. president. Letter August 4, 1812.*

> **"The annexation of Canada this year [1812]... will be a mere matter of marching."**
> ***Thomas Jefferson***

SHIFT THE BORDER. Fifty-four forty, or fight. *William Allen (1803-79). U.S. politician. The Ohio Senator's slogan became the battle cry of expansionists who wanted to extend the U.S. border to latitude 54 degrees 40 minutes north, at the southern tip of Alaska. It was the campaign cry of James K. Polk who was elected president in 1845.*

ANNEXATION. For the admission of the states of Nova Scotia, New Brunswick, Canada East and Canada West and for the organization of the territories of Selkirk, Saskatchewan and Columbia. *U.S. Congress,*

July 2, 1886. Wording of a Bill proposing the annexation of Canada.

RAILROAD FATE. The opening by us first of a North Pacific Railroad seals the destiny of British possessions west of the ninety-first meridian. Annexation will be but a question of time. *U.S. Senate, Report on Pacific railroads, February 19,1869.*

A FEW BRIBES. Nobody who has studied the peculiar methods by which elections are won in Canada will deny the fact that five or six million dollars, judiciously expended... would secure the return to Parliament of a majority pledged to the annexation of Canada to the United States. *New York World, 1890.*

A RIPE APPLE. Canada is like an apple on a tree just beyond our reach. We may strive to grasp it, but the bough recedes from our hold just in proportion to our effort to catch it. Let it alone and in due time it will fall into our hands. *James G. Blaine (1830-93), U.S. politician, secretary of state 1881 and 1889-93. Quoted by W. E. Harris in* Canada's Last Chance *(1970).*

PEAS IN A POD. You know, it seems ridiculous. We both speak the same language. We think alike. We behave the same. Don't you think you would be better off as the forty-ninth state? *Dwight Eisenhower (1890-1969), U.S. general and thirty-fourth president of the United States. Said in 1965, to Lionel Chevrier, in Washington, D.C.*

Quoted by Chevrier in St. Lawrence Seaway *(1959).*

COMMERCIAL IMPERATIVE. Sooner or later, commercial imperatives will bring about free movement of all goods back and forth across our long border; and when that occurs, or even before it does, it will become unmistakably clear that countries with economies so inextricably intertwined must also have free movement of the other vital factors of production— capital, services, labour. The result will inevitably be substantial economic integration, which will require for its full realization a progressively expanding area of common political decision. *George Ball (1909-1994), U.S. diplomat.* Discipline of Power *(1968).*

NO MEANS YES. Well, it doesn't take a Ph.D. in psychology to realize that Canadians' mock horror at the thought of becoming part of the United States actually masks a deep desire to do precisely that. They protest too much. Their lips say "no, no," but their eyes say "yes, yes." *Michael Kinsley, editor of Slate, Microsoft Corporation's on-line magazine.* Toronto Star, *December 11, 1988.*

KAPUT BORDER. This business has become a continental game. That border is kaput. *J.C. Anderson, U.S. oil man, CEO of Anderson Exploration Ltd., on Canada's booming sales of oil and natural gas to the United States, which have made Canada the largest single source of U.S. energy imports.* New York Times, *June 12, 2000.*

The mouse and the elephant

The mouse and elephant metaphor, coined by Prime Minister Pierre Elliott Trudeau, is probably the best-known metaphor for the relationship between the two countries that share North America, but others also made some sharp observations.

LIVING NEXT TO YOU [United States] is in some ways like sleeping with an elephant; no matter how friendly and even-tempered is the beast, if I may call it that, one is affected by every twitch and grunt. Even a friendly muzzle can sometimes lead to frightening consequences. *Pierre Trudeau (1919-2000), speech, Washington, May 25, 1969.*

MISSIONARY POSITION. Canada as a separate but dominated country has done as well under the U.S. as women, worldwide, have done under men; about the only position they've ever adopted toward us, country to country, has been the missionary position, and we were not on the top. *Margaret Atwood (1939-), Quoted in* If You Love this Country: Facts and Feelings on Free Trade *(1987).*

CANADA is a very nice place, and we intend to keep it that way. *John Pierpont Morgan (1837-1913), U.S. financier. Quoted by Andrew Malcolm in* The Canadians *(1985).*

> **The United States is our friend, whether we like it or not.**

OUR FRIEND. The United States is our friend whether we like it or not. *Robert Norman Thompson (1914-97), Social Credit Party leader 1961-67. House of Commons, Debates, January 31, 1963.*

CLINTON'S KNOWLEDGE. Whatever President Clinton knows about Canada, he learned from reading his briefing papers the night before. *Gordon Ritchie, Canadian public servant and trade official.* Maclean's, *February 15, 1993.*

IF AMERICANS ACQUIRE, Canadians use. Americans mythologize, Canadians pragmatize. Americans celebrate hubris, Canadian celebrate tenacity. *Advertising executive Fritz Kuhn.* Canadian Speeches, *June 1998.*

WE LIKE THE AMERICANS we know, but we do not like the United States. *Anonymous. Quoted in* Canada and her Great Neighbour, *ed. H.F. Angus (1938).*

AMERICANS don't even know we're a sovereign country here. They think we're a Guatemala or something. *Alvin Hamilton (1912-2004), Canadian Conservative politician, speech. March 6, 1963.*

IF EVER A CANADIAN wants to go to a better place all he has to do is come down to this country. But if an American wants to go to a better place, he has to die first. *Anonymous. Quoted by J. R. Kidd in a speech, Buffalo, November 5, 1959.*

I HAVE NO FEAR that the people of Upper Canada would ever desire to become the fag-end of the neighbouring republic. *George Brown (1818-80), Scottish born newspaper publisher and politician. November 10, 1859, at a Reform convention, Toronto.*

WHILE AMERICANS are benevolently ignorant about Canada, most Canadians seem malevolently informed about the United States. *Merrill Denison (1893-1975), Canadian playwright, author and historian.* Saturday Review, *June 7, 1952.*

GEOGRAPHY has made us neighbours. History has made us friends. Economics has made us partners. And necessity has made us allies. Those whom nature hath so joined together, let no man put asunder. What unites us is far greater than what divides us. *John F. Kennedy (1917-63), thirty-fifth U.S. president, Address to joint session of Parliament, 1961.*

Political lies
and other myths

FOR POLITICIANS TRUTH is a secondary-order commitment. While they should not lie, their prime function in a democracy is to persuade people why a certain course of action should be pursued. In a sense their task is to give plausible reasons for hope. *Ed Broadbent (1936-), New Democratic Leader 1975-90. Speech, Ottawa, January 27, 1995.*

DAMAGING TRUTH. There is nothing more damaging in politics than telling the truth. *A political adage cited by Bill Clinton in a television interview, Good Morning America, April 2, 2012. Clinton was referring to a statement by a Mitt Romney political staffer, implying that strong conservative views expressed by Romney in campaigning for the Republican nomination for the 2012 presidential election would later be changed during the election, should he win the nomination. Clinton suggested the staffer was speaking the truth because, referring to Romney, "That's what he's gotta do."*

RUN RIGHT, RUN LEFT. You have to run as far as you can to the right, because that's where 40 percent of the people who decide the [Republican presidential] nomi-

**There is nothing
more damaging
in politics than
telling the truth.**

nation are. And to get elected you have to run as fast as you can back to the middle, because only about four percent of the nation's voters are on the extreme right wing. *Richard Nixon (1913-94), thirty-seventh U.S. president. Letter to Senator Robert Dole on how to become president of the United States. Los Angeles Times, May 1995.*

TRUTH AND LIES. Mr. Spector told brutal, gloomy truths. Mr. Segal sees the bright side and puts an optimistic face on everything. Even political adversaries, it seems, would prefer to be lied to by Mr. Segal than told the truth by Mr. Spector. *Journalist Graham Fraser, commenting on the style and personality of two chiefs of staff in the prime minister's office, Norman Spector and his successor, Hugh Segal. Toronto* Globe and Mail, *Toronto, July 25, 1992.*

HOPE AND REALITY. When a political contest is fought between the forces of hope and the forces of reality, the people usually choose hope... Campaigns of hope... trade in the currency of emotions and feelings. Campaigns of reality rely on numbers and economic facts. *Susan Delacourt, Canadi-*

an political journalist. *Toronto* Globe and Mail, *November 27, 1995.*

PROFESSIONAL LIARS. A Senate acting as a House of Fact is essential, as an antidote for the poisoning of the democratic process by professional liars. *Philippe Deane Gigantes (1923-2004), Greek-born Canadian journalist, public servant, and senator.* The Road Ahead *(1990).*

FALSE PROMISES. Be lavish in your promises. Men prefer a false promise to a flat refusal... Contrive to get some new scandal aired against your rival, for crime, corruption, or immorality. *Advice from Quintis Cicero (102-43 BC) for his more famous brother, Marcus Cicero (106-43 BC), Roman orator and statesman, on how to get elected to the Roman Senate. Quoted by Will Durant,* The Story of Civilization, vol. 3, Caesar and Christ *(1944).*

When a political contest is fought between the forces of hope and the forces of reality, the people usually choose hope.

UNDECIDED. Mike Pearson was touring Newfoundland and there was an open-car parade in St. John's. Joey [Smallwood, Newfoundland premier] was in the back of the car with Mike, and there was a certain amount of enthusiasm being displayed on the streets of St. John's. Joey was saying, "Mike, they are all Liberals here, all Liberals." Suddenly, out of the crowd came the voice of a megaton foghorn: "Down with the bloody Liberals." A short pause, and Joey said, "I guess we will have to mark

him down as undecided." *Royce Frith (1923-), Canadian lawyer and senator. Speaking in the Senate; Senate, Debates, 1991.*

THE CAUCUS AND THE CACTUS. What is the difference between a caucus and a cactus? A cactus has all the pricks on the outside. *John Diefenbaker (1895-1979), thirteenth prime minister (1957-1963). Comment to news reporters after a caucus conspiracy in 1966 cost him his position as Progressive Conservative Party leader.*

QUICK LAW. That was the fastest I've ever seen a piece of legislation passed in this place. It just whipped by. *Rob Anders (1972-), Reform Party Member of Parliament. On legislation giving MPs a retroactive pay rise. Toronto,* Globe and Mail, *June 12, 1998.*

BRAIN POWER. Mr. Speaker, the honorable member said that he could swallow me. If he did, he would have more brains in his belly than he has in his head. *Tommy Douglas (1904-1986) Scottish-born Baptist minister, Saskatchewan premier (1944-61) and New Democratic Party Leader (1961-71).* House of Commons, Ottawa, cited in *Toronto Star, May 23, 2000.*

THE FOUNDATION of party governments is bribery, is it not? Men are party men for the spoils. They support the government of the time for the sake of the spoils. If a man "kicks" and gives an independent vote against the party he loses their patronage, does he not? Is not bribery the cornerstone of party government? *John Douglas Armour (1830-1903), Canadian Supreme Court Justice. Queen v. Bunting. Toronto* Globe, *December 5, 1884.*

BRIBES FOR ALL. We bribed them all, and generally acquired nearly everything in sight. We literally owned the Province. Public officials in Canada, so far as my experience goes, do not have that suspicious hesitancy in accepting money that characterizes some officials in this country. The Langevin crowd did not scruple to take all they could get. *Owen E. Murphy (1849-1901), U.S. businessman. Murphy was an associate of Thomas McGreevy, Member of Parliament and railway and building contractor, expelled from Parliament for political corruption and convicted of defrauding the government with bribes paid to Public Works Minister Hector Langevin and others in the government of John A. Macdonald. McGreevy was sentenced to a year in jail and Langevin was forced to resign. Interview published in* New York Times, *republished in Toronto* Globe, *November 23, 1891*

A BARNYARD PLATFORM. Once at an auction sale, my father mounted a large manure pile to speak to the assembled crowd. He apologized with ill-concealed sincerity for speaking from the Tory platform. The effect on the agrarian audience was electric. *John Kenneth Galbraith (1908-2006), Canadian-born economist, author and diplomat.* The Scotch *(1964).*

Politics is not the art of the possible. It consists in choosing between the disastrous and the unpalatable. *Galbraith.* Ambassador's Journal *(1969).*

THE IT FACTOR. When we were boys we used to stand on the corner and watch the girls go by. Some girls had IT and some didn't. Now, we could tell just like that which ones had IT and which ones didn't. And that's how you pick candidates —they've got to have IT. *George Hees (1910-1996), Canadian Progressive Conservative politician and cabinet minister. Election campaign speech, June 1962, quoted by Peter Newman in* Renegade in Power *(1963).*

LIBERALS USUALLY FISH from the sterns of rented rowboats, while Conservatives prefer to cast off the docks and let the fish come to them. Liberals tend to eat the fish they catch; Conservatives prefer to stuff them and hang them up in recreation rooms. Conservatives tend to donate their wornout clothes to the needy; Liberals wear theirs. If they see bugs, Conservatives are inclined to call for exterminators; Liberals are more likely to step on them. Conservatives usu-

> **A Senate, acting as a House of Fact, is essential, as an antidote for the poisoning of the political process by professional liars.**

ally prefer twin beds, which may contribute to the fact that Canada has more Liberals. *Peter C. Newman (1929-), Austrian-born Canadian author and editor. "How do You Tell the Difference,"* The Canadian Voter's Guide: Election 79 *(1979).*

FREELOADERS. In terms of the unemployed... don't feel particularly bad for many of these people. They don't feel bad about it themselves, as long as they're receiving generous social assistance and unemployment insurance. *Stephen Harper (1959-), 22nd prime minister. Speech, June 1997, U.S. Council for National Policy.*

Kyoto [global accord to limit greenhouse gas emissions] is essentially a socialist scheme to suck money out of wealth-producing nations. *Stephen Harper.* Toronto Star, *January 30, 2007.*

CLEAR GRIT. All sand and no dirt, clear grit all the way though. *David Christie (1818-1880), Canadian politician, founding member of the Clear Grit Party, predecessor of the Liberal Party of Canada, at a Clear Grit Convention, Markham, Ontario, March, 1850.*

WICKED TORIES. The heart of the average Tory is deceitful above all things and desperately wicked. *Alexander Mackenzie (1822-92), stonemason, newspaper editor, second prime minister of Canada, 1873-78. Speech, Clinton, Ontario, July 5, 1878.*

"What is the difference between a caucus and a cactus? A cactus has all the pricks on the outside."
John Diefenbaker.

SOBS. There are less sons of bitches in the Liberal party than in the Tory. *John W. Dafoe (1866-1944), editor of* Winnipeg Free Press *and its predecessor for 43 years. Quoted by R.L. McDougall in* Our Living Tradition *(1962).*

ISN'T IT AWFUL about those loafers sitting around taking handouts and simply sponging off the taxpayers? Let's abolish the Senate immediately. *Richard J. Needham (1912-1996), English-born Canadian journalist, columnist and author. Quoted by Allan K. McLean in the Ontario Legislature, July 23, 1992.*

OH, FOR A SENATE SEAT. I am a Liberal Conservative, or, if you will, a Conservative Liberal with a strong dash of sympathy with the Socialist idea, a friend of Labour and a believer in Progressive Radicalism. I do not desire office but would take a seat in the Canadian Senate at five minutes' notice. *Stephen Leacock, (1869-1944), Canadian economist and humourist.* The Hohenzollerns in America *(1919).*

CONSERVATIVE MILK. I know an old lady in Toronto who solemnly assured me that her Conservative cow gave two quarts of milk more each day than it had before the elections. *John A. Macdonald (1815-91), speech in Ottawa; attributed.*

SUBSIDIES. Look here, boys, a subsidy is just giving you back your own money. When governments handle it, a big chunk disappears somewhere. So why don't you just manage among yourselves. *Advice to farmers in 1948. Tom Kennedy, Ontario Minister of Agriculture. Quoted by G. Aiken in* Backbencher *(1974).*

SOMETHING IN BETWEEN. There either will be an increase or there will be no increase or there might be something in between. *Lloyd Axworthy (1939-), speaking as federal minister of employment and immigration, about the possibility of increases in the premiums for Unemployment Insurance.* Vancouver Sun, *December 11, 1993.*

We bribed them all, and generally acquired nearly everything in sight. We literally owned the province.

HOW TO KILL. If there's one thing I've learned from W.A.C. Bennett [B.C. premier 1952-72], it's how to kill. The time to hit a politician is when he's down. *Dave Barrett (1930-), speaking as British Columbia premier about his predecessor.* Maclean's, *June, 1973.*

INCOMPREHENSIBLE. It is almost incomprehensible that the vital issues of death of nations, peace or war, bankruptcy or solvency, should be determined by the counting of heads or the knowing as we do that the majority under modern conditions — happily the majority becoming smaller — are untrained and unskilled in dealing with the problems which they have to determine.

Prime Minister R.B. Bennett (1870-1947), writing in the midst of the Great Depression. Canadian Problems *(1933).*

POLITICAL THEATRE. It's all theatre; once I understood that, I was all set. *Brian Mulroney (1939-), eighteenth prime minister of Canada, 1984-1993. Comment on political life, news reports, 1991.*

SECOND BEST. Once you've been premier of New Brunswick, why would you want to be prime minister of Canada? *Frank McKenna (1948-), Canadian Liberal politician, premier of New Brunswick 1987-97.* Toronto Globe and Mail, *October 9, 1997.*

TALK FIRST, THINK LATER. Those in public life lack... opportunity of repose before engaging in public discourse. They must respond instantly, and in some cases pre-emptively, to the news. Another certainty of public debate is a corollary of the first: that those who are asked for their opinion haven't had a chance to form one. *Robert Mason Lee, Canadian journalist and author.* Toronto Globe and Mail, *Toronto, October 8, 1994.*

NO FRIENDSHIPS. You see these two guys here? If you asked them they would probably tell you they are my friends. In politics, there is no room for friendship. *Jean Chretien (1934-), prime minister 1993-210, posing for a photo with two of* *his aides, Peter Donalo and Jean Carle.* Maclean's, *February 5, 1997.*

ILL-INFORMED VOTERS. In this new era, public opinion rules. And public opinion, sadly, is often ill-informed. *Joe Clark (1939-), sixteenth prime minister of Canada, 1979-80. Toronto* Globe and Mail, *March 4, 1996.*

IGNORANT VOTERS. The great mass of the electors are ignorant & a great majority of them never read, & remain as much in the dark as to what is going on in this country as if they were residing in Europe. *Wilfrid Laurier (1841-1919), seventh prime minister of Canada, 1891-1911. Letter to Edward Blake, July 10, 1882.*

GROPING POLITICIANS. The average politician goes through a sentence like a man exploring a disused mine shaft — blind, groping, timorous and in imminent danger of cracking his shins on a subordinate clause or a nasty bit of subjunctive. *Robertson Davies (1913-95), Canadian novelist and critic.* The Papers of Samuel Marchbanks *(1986).*

MARRY A BIG PRICK. A friend suggested calling it Little Women, and I liked that, too, although it had a slightly familiar ring. The same friend suggested Talk Softly and Marry a Big Prick. *Susan Riley, Canadian journalist and author, in* Political Wives: Lives of the Saints *(1987).*

GRAVEYARD VOTERS. My boy, the only place in this world that you find unanimity is in the graveyard. And even there, I have heard it said, at election time the dead have been known to vote in various ways! *Maurice Duplessis (1890-1959), premier of Quebec 1936-39 and 1945-59. Quoted by Charles Lynch in* You Can't Print That! Memoirs of a Political Voyeur *(1983).*

CIRCUMCISED. A fully circumcised Conservative. *William Van Horne (1843-1915), U.S.-born Canadian railway builder. Quoted by John A. Macdonald in a letter to H. H. Smith, March 3, 1884, referring to the employment of Conservatives on the Canadian Pacific Railway.*

ONE CANADA. I'm a One Canada man and I've always been a One Canada man. I say the same thing from coast to coast. When I put my foot on the dog's tail in Halifax, it barks right in Vancouver. *Réal Caouette (1917-76), Quebec politician. Toronto Star, October 7, 1971.*

POLITICAL BATTLE. Politics is not a game. It is a battle. There is the difference between us. You English, you play politics. But we French, we fight politics. *Adrian Arcand (1897-1982), French-Canadian journalist and fascist.* Maclean's, *April 15, 1938.*

NWT, Archives, Northwest Territories. G-1995-001:4493

Ibyuk, the world's second largest pingo, rises like a gigantic frost heave from the Arctic coastal plain near Tuktoyaktuk.

Big and diverse

Geography

BIG. World's second biggest country with 9,093,507 square kilometres, including 9,093,507 square kilometres of land and 891,163 square kilometres of fresh water. Only Russia is bigger. At the widest point, Canada stretches 5,959 kilometres from Cape Spear, Newfoundland to the Yukon-Alaska border; north and south the spans is 4,634 kilometres from Ellesmere Island in the high Arctic to Middle Island in Lake Erie. More coastal shoreline than any other country: 93,724 kilometres. Atlantic, Pacific, and Hudson Bay shorelines account for 26,439 kilometres. Coastal island shorelines total 67,285 kilometres, largely in the Arctic.

WET. With one-quarter of the world's fresh water, Canada has more per person than any other country. It has the second largest total annual renewable water supply. Russia has about 50 percent more renewable water, but more than four times as many people. Canada has an annual renewable fresh water supply of more than 3,400 cubic kilometres; Russia has 4,500 cubic kilometres.

ICY. Glaciers cover more than two percent of Canada, an estimated 146,540 square kilometres of the Arctic Islands and 48,535 square kilometres of the mainland. These are estimates only: "At present there are no reliable figures," the national Atlas of Canada reported in 2012. But the government's Hydrology Research Institute "is in the process of identifying and measuring all glaciers in Canada." They need to do it quickly, since the glaciers are shrinking.

ROCKY. The Canadian Shield, covering more than half of Canada from the Arctic to the Great Lakes and into the northeastern United States, was the first part of North America to permanently rise above sea level. Its volcanic rocks are as old as 4.5 billion years. Beneath a thin layer of covering soil, the rocks hold one of the world's richest treasures of mineral ores—nickel, copper, zinc, iron, gold, silver, diamonds—the bedrock of Canada's mining industry.

HALF FROZEN. Almost half of Canada is frozen, covered with permafrost, ground that is permanently frozen to depths varying from about one metre to as many as 500; and up to 1,000 metres in parts of Baffin and Ellesmere islands.

PINGO! In Inuvialuktun they are known as *pinguryuaq,* says the Prince of Wales North-

ern Heritage Centre in Yellowknife. In English, they are called pingos. A pingo is a hill with a core of ice, "formed in areas of permafrost when ponds or lakes are drained. When the lake bed freezes, the ice below expands and is forced upwards." One of the world's largest concentrations of pingos— 1,350 of the hills—dramatically dot the shore of the Beaufort Sea in the Mackenzie Delta and the adjacent Tuktoyaktuk peninsula. Eight of these pingos are in the Pingo Canadian Landmark, five kilometres west of the village of Tuktoyaktuk. The largest of the eight, known as Ibyuk, rises 49 metres from the shore and stretches 300 metres in length. It is the world's second largest pingo, exceeded by one in Russia. Inuit have dug into pingos to make walk-in food freezers.

BOGGY. Muskeg—soggy areas of peat moss, grass and shrub vegetation—cover an estimated 1.3 million square kilometres of northern Canada, more than in any other country in the world. They are part of the country's wetlands that are vital to a wide range of wildlife.

FOOD LAND. Only five percent of Canada's land mass is arable land, but those 450,000 square kilometres of farm and pasture land are almost three times the total size of all of California (158,706 square kilometres); three and a half times the size of England (130,395 square kilometres;) and 150 percent the size of Italy (including Sicily and Sardinia).

HOT AND COLD. In southwestern Ontario temperatures ranged from 33⁰C

(92⁰F) to 40.6⁰C (105⁰F) for seven days in July 1936 during Canada's worst heat wave, causing 230 deaths. On February 3, 1947, Snag, Yukon saw the lowest recorded temperature in North America, -64⁰C (-83⁰F).

HUMID HEAT. Canada is the only country to use the humidex to gauge how hot it feels in the summer, based on temperature and humidity. On a humid day, if the humidex is 40 ⁰C that's what it will feel like, even if the actual temperature is only 30 ⁰C. If the humidex is 30 or higher it will cause "some discomfort;" at 40 or more, "great discomfort;" 45 is "dangerous," and 45 means heat stroke is imminent, as rated by the Meteorological Service of Canada. The United States uses a heat index based on dew point rather than relative humidity used in humidex.

WIND CHILL. The wind chill index is to winter what the humidex is to summer, the readings indicating how cold it would feel if there were no wind. Canada took the lead in developing an international standard for wind chill, hosting a global Internet workshop for 400 participants from 35 countries in April 2000. In November 2001, Canada and the United States adopted the new wind chill index, developed by scientists and medical experts from both countries. With a wind chill factor of -28 to -30 ⁰C, exposed skin can freeze in 10 to 30 minutes; five to 10 minutes at -40 to -47; two to five minutes at -48 to 54. At -55 and colder, the risk of freezing is rated "extremely high," with outdoor conditions hazardous. "Stay inside," warns the Meteorological Service.

Maid of the Mist, at the foot of Horseshoe Falls, largest of the three Niagara Falls.

MIGHTY RIVERS. Canada's rivers flow into the three bordering oceans and into what the national Atlas calls two "ocean-equivalent drainage basins," Hudson Bay and the Gulf of Mexico. Measured by the amount of fresh water dumped into an ocean, the Saint Lawrence is the largest. Stretching 3,790 kilometres and fed by big tributaries like the Ottawa, it pours fresh water into the Atlantic at an average rate of 16,800 cubic metres per second. The Mackenzie, Canada's longest river, runs 4,241 kilometers and empties into the Arctic Ocean at a rate of 9,910 cubic metres per second. The Fraser River runs 1,370 kilometres to dump 3,540 cubic metres per second into the Pacific at Vancouver.

Canada's buffalo were once almost extinct but now number more than a quarter million.

Four Canadian rivers totalling 1,675 kilometres feed into the mighty Mississippi, adding their share of Canadian water and silt to the Gulf of Mexico.

NIAGARA FALLS. Yes, it does (or, they do). While the water tumbles down at an average rate of 6,000 cubic metres per second, the falls themselves are falling back. The water erodes the soft limestone rock causing the falls to recede at a rate of more than 1.2 metres per year. They have receded more than 11 kilometres from their original position, thousands of years ago. Waterfalls are ranked by volume of water flow, and Niagara Falls rank as one of the world's greatest cataracts. But far from Canada's tallest. Della Falls on Vancouver Island, with a fall of 440 metres versus 51 metres at Horseshoe, the biggest of three Niagara Falls. But Della Falls is a trickle compared with Niagara, and doesn't rank among the world's major falls.

FLORA AND FAUNA. The great land mass and ecosystems that vary from rain forests to arid deserts, Arctic plains to lush, fruit-growing regions, endow Canada with an enormous variety of flora and fauna: some 4,100 different plants and 1,700 species of animal life, from whales to ants; from giant Douglas firs to pin-size flowers of moss campion that bloom in the high Arctic and the high Rocky Mountains of Alberta and British Columbia. Some 1,200 plants, almost a quarter of the total, have been imported, sometimes accidentally, from other regions. Non-indigenous animals include the horse, dog, cat, sheep, cattle, the brown rat and the house mouse. More than 400 wildlife—from the shaggy buffalo to Townsend's Mole—are at risk of extinction, as listed under the *Species at Risk Act.*

RETURN OF THE BUFFALO. Canada's bison—commonly called buffalo—have made a remarkable comeback. Millions once ranged from the Subarctic to Mexico, with as many as 10 million on the Canadian prairies. By the late 1800's, only a few protected prairie buffalo were left in Banff National Park, and fewer than 300 hundred of the larger wood buffalo in what is now Wood Buffalo Park. Today, there are more than 250,000 buffalo in Canada, all but fewer than 10,000 of these on hundreds of private ranches and farms, where they are raised for their meat and hides.

In 1909 and 1912, the Canadian government bought and imported a few buffalo for the Elk Island National Park in

Alberta. As the number of buffalo outgrew the Elk Island and other sanctuaries, a few were sold to farmers and ranchers, and later in increasing numbers. The largest herds in protected government sanctuaries are about 5,000 in Wood Buffalo Park, as many as 3,000 in the Northwest Territories' Mackenzie Basin Wildlife Sanctuaries, and much smaller numbers at Elk Island and Prince Albert and Grassland National Park in Saskatchewan. Buffalo meat—as with other venison—is considered healthier than beef, because it is lower in saturated fat and cholesterol.

NORTH AMERICA'S largest known collection of fossils, including dinosaur skulls, teeth and bones, is located on the shore of Bay of Fundy's Minas Basin in Nova Scotia.

PLENTIFUL PARKS. The list keeps growing, but as of 2012 Canada had 42 National Parks; 167 National Historic Sites; Four National Marine Conservation Areas; 15 UNESCO (United Nations Educational, Scientific and Cultural Organization) World Heritage sites; and hundreds of provincial and territorial parks, wildlife reserves, and historic sites. Seven of the UNESCO World Heritage sites are also National Parks or National Historic Sites. The UNESCO sites include the world's first bi-national Heritage Site: four adjacent mountain parks in the Yukon, British Columbia, and Alaska, embracing the world's largest non-polar icefields. UNESCO's Canadian Rocky Mountain Parks embrace seven parks: the Banff, Jasper, Kootenay and Yoho national parks in Alberta and British Columbia; and the Mount Robson, Mount Assiniboine and Hamber B.C. provincial parks. For information on the National Parks and Historic Sites, visit www.pc.gc.ca/progs/np-pn/index_e.asp. For UENESCO's heritage sites in Canada, visit www.whc.unesco.org/en/statiesparties/ca.

BIGGER THAN SWITZERLAND. Wood Buffalo Park, near the northeast corner of Alberta and extending into the Northwest Territories, is a pristine wilderness of northern boreal forest, plains and meadows, bisected by rivers, and overflowing with superlatives. At 44,807 square kilometres, it is Canada's largest national park, bigger than Switzerland. It is the world's second largest wildlife protection area. It has the world's largest remaining buffalo herd, the biggest beaver dam, and is home of the world's last remaining flock of North America's biggest bird, the endangered whooping crane.

MEGA ROADS. With a total length approaching one million kilometers, Canada's network of roads and highways link its far-flung communities, from the Atlantic to the Pacific, almost to the Arctic Ocean. The Trans Canada highway, at 8,030 kilometres, is the world's longest. The southern route stretches from St. John's to Victoria. A second route, the Yellowhead, branches off from the southern route in southwestern Manitoba, stretching northwest to connect Regina, Saskatoon, Edmonton, Prince Rupert and terminating at Masset, Haida Gwaii (formerly Queen Charlotte Islands.) The Dempster highway, 720 kilometres

Goat Creek Trail, a section of the Trans Canada Trail in Spray Lakes Provincial Park, Kananaskis Country, Alberta. The 22,000-kilometre recreational trail will be the world's longest.

from Dawson, Yukon to Inuvik, near the mouth of the Mackenzie River, is Canada's only year-round public highway reaching north of the Arctic Circle. It's a gravel road with no communities or services for most of the distance.

MEGA STREET. Meandering 1,896 kilometres from Lake Ontario in Toronto to Lake of the Woods, Yonge Street is the world's longest. Construction started in 1794 to link York (Toronto), the new capital of Upper Canada established by Lieutenant Governor John Graves Simcoe, with the Upper Great Lakes.

MEGA TRAIL. When completed, the Trans Canada Trail will be the world's longest recreational trail, totaling more than 22,500 kilometres. It will reach all three oceans and connect more than one thousand communities. More than 16,500 kilometres were complete by 2012, built with the funding and support of all levels of government, numerous corporations, and thousands of individual donors and volunteers. It is open for travel by foot, bicycle, horseback, canoe, and snowmobile.

NORTHERNMOST permanently inhabitant spot in the world is Alert, on the northern tip of Ellesmere Island, 817 kilometres from the North Pole. Established as a government weather station in 1950, it is now a Canadian military base.

BRIDGE OVER ICE. Confederation Bridge, spanning 12.9 kilometres to link Prince Edward Island with the Canadian mainland, is the world's longest bridge over ice-infested water. Crossing Northumberland Strait between the island and New Brunswick, the steel and concrete structure was designed to withstand ice floes and last 100 years. It was officially opened May 31, 1997. Now, when the Island is ice-bound, Islanders can no longer say, "Canada is cut off."

STANDING TALL. Toronto's CN Tower, at 553 metres, was the world's tallest free-standing structure for 30 years. In 2007 it was eclipsed by the 818-metre Burj Dubai Tower in the United Arab Emirates.

WALLED IN. Quebec City is North America's oldest walled city north of the Rio Grande, a UNESCO World Heritage Site. Originally built in 1695, these are North America's only fortified city walls that have been maintained.

POTATO FARMERS IN THE CHIPS. Potatoes are Canada's most important horticultural crop, with $846 million or one-third of all vegetable farm cash crops in fiscal 2006-07. Canadian farmers produced nearly five million tonnes and exported nearly 1.5 million tonnes of frozen French fries, seed, and table potatoes. But we are eating fewer potatoes: 76 kg per person in 1994, but only 65 kg in 2007.

NEWSPRINT BLUES. Canada is the world's largest newsprint producer. More than a quarter of the world's newspapers are printed on Canadian paper. But the industry has been hit hard by declining demand. Printed newspapers have shrunk in the era of the World Wide Web with its digital newspapers and other data. In the United States, which buys most of Canada's newsprint

Confederation bridge links New Brunswick and Prince Edward Island so that Canada is no longer cut off when Cumberland Strait is frozen.

exports, recycling of old newspapers has increased from 35 percent in 1989 to 73 percent in 2008. Revenues of Canada's newspaper mills fell from $10.9 billion in 2000 to $4.7 billion in 2009.

CANADIAN SOCIETY

DIVERSE. With one of the world's most racial, ethic, and cultural diversity, Canada is the only one in which multiculturalism is entrenched in its constitution and laws (See Chapter Twelve. Canadian diversity: A multicultural model for the world).

FOREIGN BORN. Toronto has more foreign-born residents (49.9 percent, says the 2006 national census) than any other major metropolitan centre in the world.

ECONOMIC GIANT. Canada's economy ranked ninth largest in world in 2010, says the International Monetary Fund.

WEALTHY FAMILIES. Canadians, compared to Americans, "live longer, enjoy better health…have more sex…(and) we're wealthier too," *Maclean's* reported in 2008. Later data confirm that at least our families are wealthier. Median Canadian family income in 2009 was $68,410 versus $57,000, based on average 2009 exchange rate of $1.14. Sources: Statistics Canada, U.S. Census Bureau, Revenue Canada.

QUALITY OF LIFE. Canada ranks in the top four percent of 185 nations for quality of life, according to the United Nations. Canada consistently ranked between number one and number four in the first 20 years of the UN Human Development Index, but ranked sixth in the 2011 report, behind Norway, Australia, Netherlands, the United States and New Zealand. But in quality of life data compiled in 2011 by the Organizations for Economic Co-operation and Development (OECD), Canada ranked second among 34 nations, according to an analysis by the *National Post*. Australia nudged out Canada for first place because, suggests the *Post,* of its mandatory voting laws

PEACEFUL. Canada is the eighth most peaceful of 153 countries ranked in 2011 by the Global Peace Index, ahead of such countries as Australia (18th); United Kingdom (26th); Italy (45th) and United States (82nd). Canada's homicide rate of less than 0.15 murders per 1,000 population is one-third the U.S. rate of almost 0.43 murders per 1,000.

BIG HOUSES (Or small families?) The average Canadian home has 2.5 rooms per person, more than the 2.3 rooms in the United States and an average of 1.6 rooms per person among all 34 OECD nations.

TWO NATIONAL SPORTS. In 1994, Parliament passed "An Act to declare hockey and lacrosse the national sports of Canada;" hockey the winter sport, and lacrosse the summer sport.

Insulin saves a billion lives
Birth of the oil industry

The abolition of slavery, the first European overland crossing of North America, a home of liberty and freedom for American slaves delivered on the underground railway, the birth of the global petroleum industry, a billion lives saved from premature death with the discovery of insulin. These are among Canadian achievements and inventions worth celebrating.

HIGH SOCIETY. 1605. First social club in North America established by Samuel de Champlain at Port Royal, Nova Scotia. Port Royal, France's first successful settlement in North America was founded the year before but many of the settlers died of scurvy during a bitter winter. The following year, members of Champlain's morale-boosting *l'Orde de Bon-Temps* served beaver tail, salmon, moose pie, and other wild game at Port Royal's Great Hall.

SAILBOAT. 1679 January 26. On the shore of Lake Erie, the keel is laid for the first ship built to sail the Great Lakes, the 44-tonne *Griffon.*

SHIP CANAL. 1781 February 15. First lock canal on the St. Lawrence River built by William Twiss at Coteau du Lac.

FIRST CROSSING. 1793 July 22. First Europeans to cross America, north of the Rio Grande, Alexander Mackenzie (1764-1820) and eight companions marked their trek with an inscription on a large rock at Bella Coola: "Alexander Mackenzie, from Canada, by land, the twenty-second of July, one thousand seven hundred and ninety-three." The Lewis and Clark expedition across the United States followed 13 years later.

ABOLITION. 1793 August 23. Abolition law passed by the legislature of Upper Canada prohibited importing slaves but allowed owners to retain existing slaves. Slavery was abolished in Britain and its empire in 1834 and in the United States in 1863.

SMALLPOX STOPPER. 1800. First vaccination for smallpox in North America administered by medical missionary John Clinch at Trinity, Newfoundland.

C.W. Jeffreys. From the Imperial Oil Collection.
Alexander Mackenzie and party reach Bella Coola, July 22, 1793; first Europeans to cross North America north of the Rio Grande.

UNDERGROUND RAILWAY. 1830 October 28. Josiah Henson (1789-1883), his wife and four children, ferried by rowboat across the Niagara River to Kent, Upper Canada, were among the first of as many as 90,000 American fugitive slaves to find freedom in Canada by travelling secretly by night on the "underground railway," in which they, and the "agents" who helped them, risked their lives.

STEAMSHIP. 1833 September 11. *SS Royal William,* first ship to cross the Atlantic under steam power alone, docks at Gravesend on the Thames, carrying a load of coal and seven passengers on a 25-day voyage from Pictou, Nova Scotia. The ship was built at Cape Blanc, Quebec.

COAL OIL. 1846 June 19. Nova Scotia physician, geologist and inventor Abraham

Gesner (1797-1864) demonstrates his kerosene fuel at Charlottetown. Produced initially from bitumen and coal, kerosene—a.k.a. "coal oil"—became the principal source of light for the lamps of the world for more than half a century, until the advent of Thomas Edison's electric light bulb. In 1854, a New York refinery designed by Gesner was the first to commercially produce kerosene. Within four years some 70 U.S. coal oil plants were producing "coal oil." The Gesner plant was still the largest, employing 200 men who refined 30,000 tons of coal a year to turn out 5,000 gallons of kerosene per day. The coal oil industry was short-lived but built the foundation for the petroleum industry. That awaited the discovery of North America's first commercial oil field at Oil Springs in Canada West. The coal oil refineries switched to oil to produce kerosene at much less cost.

FAST NEWS. 1849. Associated Press, established by six New York daily newspapers, relied on a complicated Canadian route for delivery of European news: by ship to Halifax; Pony Express to Digby, Nova Scotia; by steamship to Saint John, New Brunswick, and finally by telegraph to New York.

FIRST BLACK NEWSPAPER WOMAN. 1853 March. Mary Ann Shad (1823-

Abraham Gesner laid foundation of petroleum industry with process to produce kereosene.

She was editor for five years, until *The Provincial Freeman* folded permanently.

FIRST OIL COMPANY. 1854 December 18. First incorporated oil company, International Mining and Manufacturing Company, organized by prospector and mining promoter Charles Nelson Tripp (1823-1862). Chartered in Canada West (Ontario) to manufacture oils, naphtha, paints, burning fluids, varnishes and related products, its principal product was paving material, manufactured from a bitumen deposit 40 kilometres southeast of Sarnia. Tripp's bitumen won an honourable mention at the Paris Universal Exhibition in 1855 and was used to pave Paris streets. Two years later, IMM was bankrupt and Tripp returned to seek his fortune in the United States. He died in a New Orleans hotel room at age 43, reportedly of "brain congestion." His obituary said he been busy organizing companies to develop "on a gigantic scale" deposits of "oil, copper, lead, zinc and iron" that he had discovered in Louisiana and Texas.

BIRTH OF THE OIL INDUSTRY. 1858 July. Workmen digging for water near the bitumen deposit mined by Charles Tripp, found a "flow of almost pure oil," predicted to yield "not less than one thousand dollars per day of clear profit." It was North America's first commercial oil discovery, more than a year before the Titusville, Pennsylvania oil discovery launched the U.S. petroleum industry. The workers were digging for James Miller Williams (1880-1890), a Hamilton carriage maker, who refined kerosene from the bitumen before the liquid

1893) is North America's first black newspaperwoman with the 1853 publication of *The Provincial Freeman* in Windsor. The daughter of a Wilmington, Delaware shoemaker and a leader of the Underground Railway, she moved to Windsor, Canada West after the 1850 U.S. Fugitive Law threatened to return free blacks and escaped slaves in northern states to southern bondage. At Windsor, she founded a racially integrated school. When *The Voice of The Fugitive,* the leading black newspaper in Canada, attacked her ideas and character, Shad established the *Freeman*. The paper soon folded but a year later it was re-established in Toronto, later moving to Chatham.

crude oil was discovered. J.M. Williams & Co. became the world's first integrated oil company, with crude oil production, refining and marketing. Williams & Co. (later renamed Canadian Oil Company) sold its Victoria Oil kerosene in Canada, the United States, Europe and Asia for more than 20 years before it disappeared in a merger with another firm.

UNDERSEA CABLE 1858. August 16. First trans-Atlantic telegraph sent from Trinity Bay, Newfoundland to Valentia, Ireland, the culmination of undersea telegraph cable developed by Newfoundland engineer Frederick Newton Gisborn (1824-92).

ROWING CHAMPS. 1870 September 15. A four-man English rowing crew defeats the much-favoured Canadians, in a race at Montreal that drew 45,000 spectators. A year later, the Canadian crew beat the English for the world title. Ten years later, in a race on the Thames, Edward Hanlan of Toronto beat E.A. Trichett of Australia for the world's singles rowing championship with such ease that the London *Times* dubbed the race "a mere farce."

RODEO. 1872 August 28. First wild west show staged at Niagara Falls, Ontario features James Butler Hicock as "Wild Bill Hicock."

WHERE POPPIES GROW. 1915 May 3. *In Flanders Fields,* the most widely known poem of the First World War, composed in 20 minutes by Dr. John McCrae (1872-1918) of Guelph, Ontario.

The Red Baron, Germany's top First World War air ace, was shot down in a dogfight by Canadian airman Roy Brown.

A PAIR OF AIR ACES. 1918 April 21. The Red Baron, Manfred von Richthofen, Germany's top First World War air ace, shot down in a dogfight by Canadian airman Roy Brown (1893-1944). William Avery "Billy" Bishop (1894-1956) was Canada's top air ace in the war, shooting down 72 enemy aircraft, exceeded among allied forces only by French aviator Rene Fonck, who shot down 75.

MUSICAL RADIO. 1918 December. First music broadcast by radio transmitted by Marconi Wireless Telegraph Co. of Canada from Montreal to the Chateau Laurier Hotel in Ottawa.

BLUENOSE. 1921 March 26. Canada's most famous ship, launched at Lunenburg, Nova Scotia. The 40-metre schooner won four of six contests for the International Fisherman's Trophy from 1921 to 1938. *Bluenose* was sold in 1942 to a West Indies trading company, hauling scrap, and wrecked in 1946 after hitting a reef off Haiti. A replica, *Bluenose II,* was launched in 1963.

NO BATTERIES. 1925 April 08. First radio to operate on common household electric AC power, in place of batteries, built by Edward Samuel Rogers (1889-1953) and his two chief engineers. To promote sales of his radio, Rogers established Toronto radio station CFRB, which stood for "Canada's First Rogers Batteryless."

WAR MEDICINE. 1936. Battlefield medical care is revolutionized by Canadian physician Norman Bethune (1890-1939) with the development of the first mobile blood transfusion service, while serving as a medical officer with Republican forces during the Spanish civil war.

SUPERMAN. 1939 January. The comic book hero is born in the pages of *Action Comics*, the creation of Toronto-born artist Joe Shuster (1914-1992) and writer Jerome Siegal. Receiving very little financial reward for their creation, they were impoverished for years. A copy of the first issue of *Action Comics* with the Superman was sold in 2010 at an auction for $1. 5 million.

PILOT TRAINING. 1939 December 17. Air crews from Britain, Australia, New Zealand and Canada to be trained in Canada by RCAF for service in Second World War, under the British Commonwealth Air Training Plan. By war's end, 130,000 airmen had been trained.

Superman creators Joe Shuster and Jerome Siegal remained impoverished but a copy of this first issue of *Action Comics,* 1939, sold at an auction in 2010 for $1.5 million.

JET TRANSPORTER. 1949 August 10. Inaugral flight of the AVRO C102, North America's first jet transport aircraft, built by Avro Canada in Malton, Ontario. The C102 flew for seven years, setting many records.

SWIMMING CHAMPS. 1954 September 9. Toronto's 16-year-old Marilyn Bell is the first to swim across Lake Ontario, from Youngstown, New York to Toronto, a distance of 54 kilometres. Twenty years later, Cindy Nicholas, also of Toronto, sets the speed record for swimming across the lake in 15 hours and 18 minutes, beating the previous record by almost three hours. In 1977, Nicholas set the record for a non-stop return swim across the English Channel, beating the previous record by almost 10 hours.

OIL SANDS. 1967 September 25. Start of synthetic crude oil production from the world's largest petroleum deposit, the Athabasca oil sands in northern Alberta. By 2015, the oil sands are expected to account for one-fifth of all North American oil production.

UNDERGROUND WALK. 1967 December 06. World's longest underground walkway, 4.8 kilometres, opened in Montreal. It connects Place Ville Marie, Place Bonaventure, and Central Station.

EYE SURGERY. 1968 November 06. Toronto surgeons perform first plastic cornea implant in a human eye.

DIGITAL TALK. 1973 January 19. Dataroute, world's first commercial digital telecom system, inaugurated by Trans-Canada Telephone System.

SPACE ARM. 1983 June 22. Canadarm is used on a U.S. space shuttle for the first release and recovery of a satellite in space.

CANCER HIKE. 1985 May 29. Steve Fonyo, a one-legged cancer victim, dips artificial leg in the Pacific Ocean after completing a 14-month, fund-raising walk across Canada. Terry Fox attempted the feat in 1980 but was forced to halt his journey in Sudbury after cancer had spread to his lungs.

BASEBALL CHAMPS. 1992 October 24. Toronto Blue Jays team becomes first non-American team to win the World Series title, defeating Atlanta Braves in game six. The Jays won the title again the following year.

ICE BREAKER. 2006. *MV Umiak I,* world's most powerful ice-breaker bulk carrier, is launched in Japan for Fednav Limited of Montreal, to haul nickel concentrates from the Voisey Bay mine in Labrador to Quebec City. Its 30,000 hp diesel engine is designed to break through ice as thick as 20 metres. From Quebec the concentrate is moved by railway to Sudbury for refining.

EASY RIDER. 2009 July 28. Fastest bicycle trip across Canada, Vancouver to St. John's, completed by Cornel Dobrin. of Langley, B.C. Dobrin made the trip in 27 days, 5 hours and 30 minutes, beating the previous record by more than one day.

A FEW INVENTIONS

HELLO! 1876 March 10. Alexander Graham Bell's telephone launched in Boston, when Bell calls his assistant in a nearby room, "Mr. Watson, come here, I want to see you." On August 3, Bell made the first 'phone call between two buildings at Mount Pleasant, Ontario; and on August 10, the first long-distance call, 13 kilometres, from Brantford to Paris, Ontario.

CHECK YOUR CLOCKS. 1879 February 8. Standard time, dividing the world into 24 zones, proposed by Sanford Fleming (1827-1915) to end the chaos of varying local times. His Standard Time was adopted by all North American railways in 1883 and implemented by 25 countries on January 1, 1885.

SLAM DUNK! 1892 December 15. First game of basketball—invented by Canadian physician and physical education instructor James A. Naismith (1861-1939)—played in the gymnasium of the YMCA International Training School in Springfield, Massachusetts, using peach baskets nailed to the balconies at either end of the gym.

SNOWMOBILE. 1922. Fifteen-year-old Joseph-Armand Bombardier builds world's first snowmobile: a sled with a Ford model T engine that drove a rear-mounted wooden aircraft-type propeller. His father orders it dismantled, fearing that the propeller is too dangerous. In 1935 Bombardier built the first commercial snowmobile, in Valcourt, Quebec, a track-driven passenger vehicle steered by skis in the front, the prototype of vehicles that revolutionized travel in snow, swamp and muskeg conditions in oil, mining, and forestry operations. In 1959, Bombardier built a one- or two-passenger snowmobile intended for use by hunters and trappers as an alternative to dogsleds. He called his new machine Ski-Dogs but a painter misread the instructions and painted Ski-Doo on the first machines.

A BILLION LIVES SAVED. 1922 February 11. Discovery of insulin announced. Patent rights were soon sold for $1 to the University of Toronto, to make the new diabetes treatment widely and cheaply available. The discovery was made by medical researchers Frederick Banting (1891-1941), Charles Best (1899-1978), James Collip (1892-1965) and James Macleod (1876-1935). Ninety years later, almost 300 million people worldwide were diabetic, of whom about a quarter, or some 70 million, were treated with insulin. Insulin is thought to have saved as many as one billion lives from premature death.

MORE INVENTIONS

1797: McIntosh apple, John McIntosh...**1833:** Ship screw propeller, John Patch. Newsprint, Charles Fenerty...**1854:** Odometer, Samuel McKeen... **1857:** Railway sleeper car, Samuel Sharp... **1858:** Air-conditioned railway coach, Henry Ruttan... **1859:** Automatic foghorn, Robert Foulis... **1862:** Green currency ink (causing U.S. dollar to be called a greenback), Thomas Sterry Hunt... **1869:** Half-tone engraving, Georges Edourad and William Leggo... **1869:** Rotary railroad snowplow, J.E. Elliott... **1882:** Electric car heater, Thomas Ahearn... **1889:** Gramophone, Alexander Graham Bell and Emile Berliner... **1890:** Electric cooking range, Thomas Ahearn... **1900:** Wireless radio, Reginald A. Fessenden... **1904:** Acetylene, Thomas L. Wilson... **1908:** Hydrofoil boat, Alexander Graham Bell and Casey Baldwin... **1909:** Five-pin bowling, Thomas F.Ryan. **1913:** Zipper, Gideon Sundback... **1925:** Snowblower, Arthur Sicard. Wirephoto, Edward Samuel Rogers... **1928:** Electric organ, Morse Robb... **1934:** Television camera, F. C. P. Henroteau... **1937:** Electron microscope, Cecil Hall, Eli Franklin Burton, James Hiller, and Albert Prebus... **1940:** Paint roller, Norman Breakey... **1941.** Anti-gravity suit, Wilbur Rounding Franks...**1942.** Walkie-Talkie, Donald L. Hings... **1950:** Heart-pacemaker, John A. Hopps... **1957:** Analytical plotter, 3D map-making system, Uno Vilho Helava... **1959:** Jolly Jumper, Olivia Poole... **1960:** Bone marrow compatibility test, Barbara Bain... **1971:** Electric Prosthetic Hand, Helmut Lucas... **1971:** Ultraviolet degradable plastic, James Guillet... **1972:** Computerized Braille, Roland Galarneau... **1990:** Explosives Vapour Detector, Dr Lorne Elias.

Rick Hansen wheels around the world

Thousands of cheering supporters greeted 30-year-old Rick Hansen at Vancouver's B.C. Place Stadium, May 22, 1987, as he pushed his wheelchair the final yards of a 26-month, 40,073-kilometre journey, crossing four continents, 34 countries, and five mountain ranges.

As a teenage athlete, Hansen won all-star awards in five sports. That ended two-months before his sixteenth birthday, when he was paralyzed from the waist down. A pickup truck, in which he was riding in the back, crashed, breaking his back and severing his spinal cord. After extensive rehabilitation and becoming the first person with a disability to earn a degree in physical education from the University of British Columbia, he earned distinction as one of the world's top Paralympians.

Between 1979 and 1984, he won 19 international wheelchair marathons, including the world title three times. He was the first to break the two-hour time in a wheelchair marathon. He won gold, silver and bronze medals at the 1980 Paralympic summer games; and nine gold medals at the 1982 Pan Am Games, including wheelchair volleyball, and basketball.

Raising money was never the real purpose of his epic journey. "The greatest impact," he has said, "was and always will be the human side of the mission… to inspire people… to think differently about what is

Rick Hansen Foundation

Rick Hansen in Man in Motion World Tour, Salem, Oregon, 1987.

possible for anyone when barriers are removed, attitudinal or physical."

Donations still rolled in, amounting to $26 million by the end of the tour. Twenty-five years later, Rick Hansen and the Rick Hanson Foundation had raised and donated more than $200 million for spinal cord injury research, and quality of life and motivational programs.

Joyce Hill, Wikimedia Commons

Replica Viking ships approach L'Anse aux Meadows National Historic Site in 2000 reenactment of arrival of the first Europeans to establish a settlement in North America.

Vikings in Newfoundland

Christopher Columbus was a century or so late in "discovering America," when he arrived in 1492. Ireland's St. Brendan, with some 60 pilgrims, sailed across the Atlantic between 565 and 572 in open ox-hide boats called currachs to a land he called Paradise, thought to be Newfoundland, according to several written legends.

The story is feasible. There is no dispute that the Irish had sailed their currachs to settle as far as Iceland. British adventurer Tim Severin built a replica currach and sailed it from Ireland to Newfoundland in 1976-77. But there is no conclusive evidence of St. Brendan's voyage. Another legend has Irish monks sailing from Iceland in 875 to settle first in the Magdalen Islands in the Gulf of the St. Lawrence, and then on Cape Breton Island. Later Norse explorers called the area the country of the white man. If the monks did settle here, they left no evidence to confirm their presence.

Vikings sailing from Iceland for Greenland were the first confirmed Europeans to sight Newfoundland, and possibly Labrador and Baffin Island, in 985 when their ship, enroute to Iceland, was blown off course. A decade later, Leif Ericsson became the first confirmed European to set foot on mainland North America, setting up a camp on what he called Vinland, somewhere near the Gulf of St. Lawrence. Ericsson and his men remained for about a year before returning to Greenland with wine, vines and lumber.

About 1,004, a flotilla of four ships, with 160 men (and at least one woman) plus cattle, landed near Anse aux Meadows on the northern tip of Newfoundland at what is now a United Nations World Historic site, marking the first confirmed European settlement in North America.

The settlement included eight timber and turf houses (the largest 19 by 14 metres), a forge, and four workshops. Gudrid, the wife of the colony's leader, Thorfinn Karlsefni, gave birth here to a son, Snorri, the first child born in North America of European parents. The Vikings stayed at Anse aux Meadows for three or four years, and continued further exploration, before returning to Greenland.

This marked the end of Viking exploration of North America, possibly because the Little Ice Age was making the region less hospitable, or because all the land the Vikings needed was available at Greenland and Iceland, or because North America seemed to offer nothing that was not more readily available from Norway.

Almost four hundred years went by before the next Europeans are reputed to have visited Canada—a century before Columbus. Harry Sinclair, the Scottish Earl of Rosslyn, with 12 ships and 300 men, is claimed to have landed at what is now Guysborough, Nova Scotia, on June 12, 1398, and spent some time exploring the peninsula. While the claim is staunchly advocated, conclusive evidence is still lacking.

After the Vikings, British-Italian explorer John Cabot was the first to land in North America, in 1497. Christopher Columbus landed in the the Bahamas in 1492, and in South America in 1498. Cabot landed in either Newfoundland, Labrador, or Cape Breton.

Whoever were the first Europeans to visit Canada they were far from the first to "discover" North America. Native Americans arrived from Asia thousands of years earlier, and there were anywhere from 40 million to 100 million of them when the Europeans arrived.

First Europeans arrived 40 million years after native North Americans.

The myth of the Plains of Abraham and the Conquest of Canada

B ritish General James Wolfe is widely proclaimed as having cast the destiny of Canada with the defeat of Louis-Joseph Montcalm and the French on the Plains of Abraham, September 13, 1759. Not so. The destiny not only of Canada but North America was cast on the far side of the Atlantic, in a pair of events that many histories have ignored or overlooked.

With periodic outbreaks of peace, the French and English began fighting each other for control of North America almost as soon as their first settlers landed. The shooting started in 1613 when Virginia Company sea captain Samuel Argall and Virginia colonials attacked the French Jesuit Mission on the Îsle Monte Désert, off the northern end of Maine. In a second attack that year, Argall sacked every building in Port Royal—seven years after the first French settlers arrived there; six years after the first English settled at Jamestown; five years after the French at Quebec.

Now, 141 years later, the stage is set for the final conflict.

It is 1754, and the French claim the most territory. New France sprawls over the heart and length of the continent, from Labrador and the Gulf of the St. Lawrence to the Gulf of Mexico. It is home for possibly 80,000 people: half of them in Canada, straddling either side of the St. Lawrence for a distance of 400 kilometres; the rest in Acadia, mostly present day New Brunswick; and in Louisiana with its New Orleans. The English have far more people, 1.2 million in colonies on the Atlantic seaboard between Acadia and Spanish Florida.

"A volley fired by a young Virginian in the backwoods of America, set the world on fire," as Horace Walpole noticed. The young Virginian was 22-year-old militia captain George Washington. He came to the Ohio Valley on behalf of speculators and their Ohio Company, which had been granted

200,000 acres, nominally by generous King George II, in territory the French claimed lay within their New France. To protect their fur traders and prospective settlers, the Virginians built a small fort at what is now Pittsburgh. The French sent troops to stop the English trading with the Indians and establish settlements. Washington was dispatched with a small troop and orders to restrain French obstruction, "and in case of resistance to make prisoners of or kill and destroy them." At daybreak on May 28, the future U.S. president, his troops, and a few warriors swept down on a camp of 31 sleeping Canadien militia, killing 10.

"A volley fired by a young Virginian in the backwoods of America, set the world on fire."

Two years of undeclared war in North America had started. This was the first phase of the global Seven Years' War that pitted England and its allies against France and its allies. By the time it was over, 1.4 million people were killed in fighting in North America, Europe, Africa, Asia, India, and the West Indies. Winston Churchill called it the first world war.

England and France sent shiploads of soldiers across the Atlantic to join the fight in North America. The certain losers were the First Nations. Mohawk Chief Hendrick told a conference of colonial governors at Albany:

"The Governor of Virginia and the Governor of Canada are both quarrelling about land which belongs to us, and such a quarrel as this may end in our destruction: they fight who shall have the land." The Europeans took no heed.

We need not detail all the North American battles—Oswego, Fort William Henry, Monongahela, Ticonderoga, Fort Frontenac (Kingston), Fort Duquesne (Pittsburgh), and more—before the shooting stopped, except to briefly note two. At the instigation of New England land speculator, the British captured what remained of French Acadia, i.e., present day New Brunswick, and began the historic expulsion of more than 11,000 Acadians to distant lands. In 1758, the British captured Louisbourg, the French fortress on Cape Breton Island that guarded the St. Lawrence gateway to Canada. James Wolfe was in the thick of that action, leading the Fraser Highlanders. Wolfe and the Highlanders sailed the next year for what historian D. Peter Macleod has called, "The battle that would decide the fate of Canada and the French and British Empires in North America."

Quebec, the key to New France, might have fallen without a shot, if a British fleet had acted more promptly to cut off a daring exploit by a Canadien butcher.

"We could perish from lack of food without firing a shot," Louis-Joseph Montcalm, New Frances' military leader warned in early 1759 as Quebec prepared for an anticipated British invasion. Food shortages seemed a graver threat than the British. Heavy rains and cold weather had yielded poor crops. There was not enough food to

Devastation of Quebec by Wolfe's artillery during siege of 1759, as depicted by artist Richard Short.

feed Quebec's civilians and armed forces until more might come in the summer from the more fertile fields of Montreal, 130 kilometres upstream. Pierre de Vaudreuil, the first Canadian-born governor of New France, asked France for a large shipment of provisions and arms. France was too preoccupied with the British navy, on the other side of the Atlantic, to offer much help.

Joseph-Michel Cadet secured the needed provisions in France, and chartered a private fleet of supply ships and two armed frigates to bring them to Quebec. Cadet learned the butcher trade from his uncle; started a butcher shop, added wheat, flour, peas, and biscuits to his business; won a nine-year contract as purveyor general of Canada. With a string of warehouses and 4,000 employees, he was possibly the wealthiest man in New France, and seemingly undeterred by any risk.

While Cadet was organizing his food convoy, British Rear Admiral Philip Durell was ordered to sail with his fleet, harboured at Halifax, to blockade the St. Lawrence as soon as the breakup of ice permitted. Wolfe was less than pleased when he learned that Durell would be in charge of the blockade, describing the admiral as "vastly unequal to the weight of the business."

In late March, Durell sent small ships to survey ice conditions in the Gulf of St. Lawrence. By April 8, his warships were ready to sail. Ostensibly because of ice conditions and bad weather, it was a month later, May 5, before Durell and his fleet set sail from Halifax.

Too late!

By the time Durell's fleet was in position to block the river, Cadet's navy had delivered their provisions to Quebec. The French navy came through with at least token support: one supply ship and two frigates. With short rations, Quebec had enough food to last until August. Food remained on short rations and lack of supplies a constant threat, but Cadet overcame formidable obstacles to keep Quebec on life support for 18 months.

The fortress city

For a fortified city, a more impregnable site than Quebec is difficult to imagine. It perches at the apex of a 15-kilometre plateau, edged by steep banks that rise 50 to 90 metres from three rivers: the mighty St. Lawrence, along the length of the plateau, narrowed at Quebec to little more than two kilometres; the smaller St. Charles to the north and Cap Rouge to the south. Only the western edge of the city lacked the barrier of a steep bank. In its place was the wall, six metres of solid stone and mortar, 12 metres high, stretching across the plateau. Upper Quebec, housing most of city, its army, its administrative and business buildings, its splendid cathedral, looks down on Lower Quebec, hugging a narrow shoreline.

Across the St. Charles River the Beauport Flats shoreline stretches invitingly for 10 kilometres. Montcalm is convinced that the Beauport shore is "the only place where the enemy can, and must, make their landing." He has built his defence here: entrenchments for thousands of soldiers backed by artillery batteries, well positioned to fire muskets and cannons on any force foolhardy enough to try a landing. He dismissed the possibility of an attack landing against the steep banks upstream from the city. "We don't have to believe that the enemy has wings that allow him to cross [the river], disembark, and climb over the city walls," he assures Governor Pierre Vaudreuil. Throughout the coming three-month siege, few of Montcalm's forces guard 60 kilometres of upstream; most remain entrenched along the Beauport Flats, with a garrison behind the city wall, in case an enemy should ever reach that far. Montcalm has made his first mistake.

The St. Lawrence south shore, opposite Quebec, is left unguarded. Montcalm did not believe the British could bombard the city from a distance of close to two kilometres. Another mistake.

With tricky navigation in the narrowed St. Lawrence opposite Quebec, planted with false navigation aids, Montcalm felt confident that no large British warships could get upstream past the city, between Quebec and its vital food supplies from Montreal, and to where a large cache of guns and ammunition had been stockpiled for safe keeping. Yet another miscalculation.

The armies

There were more armed forces than unarmed

civilians in Canada at the start of the prolonged conquest: 48,000 soldiers and sailors, as estimated by the National Battlefields Commission, close to double the number of children, old folks, and women.

Montcalm had an armed force of about 19,000, double Wolfe's 9,000 troops, although estimates of Montcalm's forces vary significantly. The British also had 20,000 sailors aboard 320 large and small ships. More than half of Montcalm's forces were part-time soldiers, poorly trained and ill equipped. Wolfe's troops were full-time professionals, well equipped, tightly disciplined, endlessly trained and drilled whenever not fighting.

Montcalm had about 6,000 full-time armed forces: 2,400 regular troops from France; 2,000 land-based navy artillery and infantry; 1,000 or more Troupes de la Marine. Montcalm also had 11,000 part-time militia soldiers, and as many as 1,800 First Nations warriors. Montcalm had no faith in the effectiveness of the militia, and not much more in the incongruously named "Troops of the Navy." They had long since ceased to be an active party of any navy; they were land-based

Land claims in 1754, after 141 years of fighting by the English and French for control of North America. The final conflict lasts another six years, but the outcome is determined on the far side of the Atlantic.

companies of full-time guerrilla and bush fighters, led by Canadian-born officers and largely staffed by Canadiens. Despite Montcalm's misgivings, they were skilled and highly effective in ambushing and harassing the flanks of British armies. Montcalm's militia supposedly embraced every able-bodied male civilian in Canada between ages 16 and 60. But if the Battlefield Commission's estimate of 11,000 is near the mark, the ranks most likely included younger teenagers and perhaps some 60 older than 60.

The English, who formed the bulk of Wolfe's troops, likely included many who were there through "sheer necessity." Gloucestershire was one of five "shires" from which the English troops were recruited. Three years earlier, Wolfe had been sent to Gloucester to quell rioting weavers. He hoped, he wrote, to secure "a good recruiting party, for the people are so oppressed, so poor and so wretched, that they will perhaps… turn soldiers through sheer necessity." Gloucester was not the only pocket of poverty in England.

Many of the Scots who formed Wolfe's largest regiment, the 78th Fraser Highlanders, were likely there for the same reason as the English. Their commanding officer, Simon Fraser was chieftain of the clan from which he recruited 1,500 members for the regiment. He was there to further his own interests. Twelve years earlier, his clansmen fought the English in the Battle of Culloden that killed the hope of an independent Scotland. Now—reduced to 1,200 after serving in the siege of Louisbourg—they were in Canada to fight once more for the English.

American colonists, from the seaboard south of Acadia, were 3,000 strong, one-third of Wolfe's army. They were natural allies of the British: they did not like the prospect of being ruled by a French-speaking, Catholic monarchy, especially one which stood athwart their territorial ambitions, and they had inducements of pay and the prospect of land grants. Once the French were kicked out of North America, the colonists would be free to kick out the English, which they set out to do 16 years after the Conquest of Canada.

The long siege

The British armada arrived in mid-June, carrying troops, guns, ammunition, and enough food—including 591 cattle—to feed some 29,000 men. They set up their first camp within sight of the city, on the evacuated Île d' Orléans, commandeering the church for their field hospital.

The first three months of the siege were a stalemate. For the British it was a frustrating time of failure to entice the French into an open-field pitched battle; a failed attack at Montmorency Falls; of searching for another point of attack; of disease and sickness that thinned the ranks; of ceaseless artillery pounding of Quebec; and a terror campaign of burning and pillage along the undefended south shore. Montcalm remained largely ensconced behind his fortifications.

When Wolfe found that his plan of launching an attack at the Beauport Flats had been rendered impossible by Montcalm's defence, he vowed a campaign of terror. "[If] we find that Quebec is not likely to fall into our hands… I propose to set the town on fire with Shells, to destroy the Harvest, Houses & cattle, both above and below, to send off as many Canadians as possible to Europe, & to leave famine and desolation behind me," Wolfe wrote to General Jeffrey Amherst, commander of British forces in North America.

Artillery commander George Williamson established a large battery of guns on the south shore at the closest point to Quebec: 20 cannon that shot solid iron balls weighing up to 14.5 kilogram (32 pounds), and 13 mortars that shot flaming firebombs to burn the city. Only about a fifth of Quebec's buildings were made of wood, but the stone buildings had wooden roofs. The shelling began in mid-July. By the time it was over, most of the city lay in rubble. The city was evacuated. A few remained to stop looting, put out fires, safeguard stores and provisions. The evacuees did not have far to go. The artillery range was 1,200 to 1,800 yards, according to Williamson. The stone wall on the far side of the city was 2,200 yards away. It remained intact. Safe, too, was the general hospital, more than a kilometre past the city wall, a haven for civilians and soldiers alike, and later for British soldiers.

Under cover of darkness and heavy bombardment by Williamson's artillery, five British warships, commanded by Rear Admiral Charles Holmes, slipped upstream past Quebec, undetected. Soldiers marched along the south shore to join the fleet. The British now stood athwart Quebec and its Montreal food supply. Wolfe is positioned to launch an amphibious attack either upstream or downstream from Quebec. Montcalm is compelled to pay more attention to guarding the upstream shoreline. As many as 2,000 are sent to patrol it, marching up and down along the banks, following the movement of British warships that were

Wolfe vows to set Quebec on fire, destroy harvest, houses and cattle, and "leave famine and desolation behind me."

not supposed to be there. Some of the upstream forces are later sent back to the Beauport Flats, where Montcalm remains convinced the attack must come.

Wolfe's first amphibious attack comes from the downstream side of Quebec, at Montmorency Falls, on the flank of the fortifications along the Beauport Flats. It is a disaster. The British charge uphill, to be mowed down by entrenched French forces. The British suffer 210 killed; 233 wounded. The French suffer 60 casualties.

The terror campaign on undefended villages begins upstream from Quebec when Admiral Charles Holmes launches small amphibious attacks on four villages on either side of the river. The first attack is repelled with British losses. On the other attacks, his forces burn a storehouse of weapons and ammunition, disperse a few warriors, and slaughter more than 100 cattle and sheep. Two villages on the south shore that pose no military threat are torched; every house in the perish of Saint-Croix is burned.

Wolfe assigns American Major George Scott to a much greater terror campaign, with orders to "burn all the country" along 120 kilometres of the south shore until it "is totally destroyed." Scott leads a force of 600 American Rangers and 1,000 light infantry, supported by a small fleet of warships. They burn crops, houses, barns and almost every building in sight, kill cattle and horses, imprison old men, women and children. At Rivierè Ouelle, the manor house, flourmill, sawmill and fishing boats of a prosperous seignior are turned to charred wrecks and ashes. At another site, a woman nine months pregnant was forced to flee into the forest where she gave birth to a baby on a bed of leafs. Not surprisingly, Canadiens who had not been conscripted into the militia fired pot shots with their farm muskets, causing a few casualties. One Ranger was scalped.

With hot summer days and poor camp sanitation, diarrhea, dysentery and typhus claimed numerous lives and left more than 1,000 too sick to fight. That, plus fighting casualties at Montmorency Falls and 1,600 troops marauding the south shore, left Wolfe with just 6,000 of his original 9,000 available for the siege of Quebec. Wolfe, too, was laid low with a fever, fell into despair and despondency, while his generals and brigadiers fell to arguing and criticizing his military leadership. But Wolfe recovered to take firm control. There was general agreement that an attack should be made upstream from Quebec, but no agreement just where that should be. Wolfe finally made the decision. It would be "where the enemy seems least to expect it."

The Anse au Foulon lies at the foot of a steep, 53-metre, heavily-wooded bank, a little more than two kilometres from Quebec. A road from the cove runs diagonally across the bank up to the Plains of Abraham. A barrier of sorts has been placed across the road: a trench and a bramble barricade of logs and sharp, pointed branches. It is lightly guarded. Thirty gunners man the Samos battery of three small cannon and one mortar over-looking the cove from the upstream side. No more than 100 troops guard the landing site and the barricade, and patrol the top of the bank.

September 12 finds many of the French confident that they have withstood the siege, "invincible" behind the entrenched Beauport Flats. The British have been noted moving about. The camp at Montmorency has been removed. The British must be preparing to leave. "Everyone considered the campaign to have finished, and finished gloriously for us, the enemy up until then had done nothing but make useless attacks," a senior staff officer later recalled.

Not quite so. Time and tide can turn fortune or misfortune. At Cap Rouge, 15 kilometres upstream from Quebec, two parties awaited an ebb tide that will turn on the first hours of September 13 to carry their craft silently downstream. Close to shore are 19 bateaux, loaded with 4,500 litres of flour and wheat that Cadet has brought from Montreal. They are urgently needed at Quebec. Ready to weigh anchor midstream are 30 British landing craft, three sloops and four battleships, scheduled to carry 4,400 troops, field cannons, and ammunition to Anse au Foulon.

The British are informed of the planned food shipment, reportedly by a pair of French deserters, or possibly captives. In the event, the food bateaux never leave Cap Rouge. No matter. The British put their knowledge of the planned shipment to good use.

The 30 landing craft, crammed with the troops, start out at 2:20 a.m., the other vessels following during the next hour. It is 4 a.m. and dimly light when the first landing craft comes abreast of the Samos Battery. It is challenged by a French sentry. A Scot with the Fraser Highlanders replies in perfect French that these are the vessels with the food for Quebec. The reply comes from either Captain Donald MacDonald or Captain Simon Fraser; historians differ. It does not come from Lieutenant Colonel Simon Fraser, the regiment commander who missed the Battle of Culloden 12 years ago. He now misses the Battle of the Plains of Abraham. He is in the church at Saint Laurent on Île d' Orléans that serves as the British field hospital, convalescing.

The ebb tide sweeps the landing craft half a kilometre past the intended landing site—fortunately for the British. The first soldiers leap ashore at 4:07 a.m., under the fire of the guns at the Samos Battery and the muskets of the guard troops. The attackers suffer their first casualties, but are only a few steps from the forest where they are less exposed than if they had landed where originally intended. In fewer than 15 minutes the first troops have ascended the bank, attacked from the rear and silenced the Samos battery. The French troops continue to fire their muskets at the British. The shooting has started and is almost continuous throughout most of the day, even though the pitch battle lasts only minutes.

By early morning, Wolfe's army was established on the Plains of Abraham; the Foulon Road has been cleared; the first cannons hauled up for a field battery; entrenchments dug. Wolfe is positioned on a small hill with a view of the battlefield. He has 2,100 troops arranged two-abreast on the front battle line, across the width of the plain; others are shooting back at the militia and warriors who harass his flanks; the rest are held in reserve.

Facing the British, Montcalm stands on a wooded hill, the Buttes-À-Neveu, with 2,000 regular troops, about to disobey an order from Governor Vaudreuil, who is also commander-in-chief of French forces in New France. Vaudreuil and Montcalm were seldom in agreement. Montcalm was a careful, methodical, somewhat cautious military leader. Vaudreuil, a seasoned soldier, was an aggressive fighter, constantly itching to be on the attack. Now the roles are somewhat reversed. Vaudreuil ordered Montcalm to wait on his hill for the arrival of reinforcements; 1,200 militia upstream at Cap Rouge under the command of Colonel Louis-Antoine de Bougainville; 1,500 from the Beauport Flats; 2,000 standing guard within the city gates, in case they are needed for a last-ditch stand. The British, claimed Vaudreuil, would thus "find themselves surrounded on all sides, and would have no alternative but to retreat or face certain defeat."

Montcalm saw it differently. "We cannot avoid action," he reportedly told an artillery officer. "The enemy is entrenching, he al-

Montcalm disobeys an order; does not wait for reinforcements before starting battle.

ready has two pieces of cannon. If we give him time to establish himself, we shall never be able to attack him with the troops we have." He placed little value on help from the militia; he relied on his regular troops from France, massed on the hill, and ready to go.

Montcalm gave the order at 10 a.m. It was not an orderly advance. Over-eager troops rushed pell-mell down the rugged hill, through bush and wheat fields, jumping over fences. They formed a ragged line, 120 metres from the British. Without waiting for an order, the French began firing. The range was too far. Most bullets fell to the ground, others hit with such little force that they caused no damage.

The two sides approach to within less than 35 yards, the French spread out in three clustered formations, the British in a solid line. They stand for as long as two minutes, each side waiting for the other to fire first. The French fire first, causing relatively few casualties. The British response is more deadly. In dense smoke from musket fire, the shooting continues for about another 10 minutes. The French fight against the overwhelming power of British cannon and musket firing, suffering heavy casualties before retreating in a route that becomes a panic. Wolfe and Montcalm are among the casualties. Wolfe dies on the battlefield; Montcalm dies the next morning inside the city gates.

While the French soldiers of the battle line broke and ran, the Canadian militia and the warriors continued to harass the British. From the big hill, they covered the fleeing French soldiers. On the northern edge of the battlefield, the militia inflicted heavy losses on the Fraser Highlanders.

The British and the French each suffered about 600 casualties on the Plains of Abraham.

The French army lost the battle but the British had not yet taken Quebec. Fewer than 500 soldiers and sailors remained in the city to defend it, together with 2,700 refugees who fled there for safety. For four days, the British prepare to launch an attack. The French fire back, but to little effect. The British dig their entrenchments and mount their batteries. They were preparing to bomb an opening through the city's wall, then pour in for a fight that would cause great casualties on both sites. It would be a blood bath that neither the British nor the French really wanted.

From his camp at the Jacque Cartier River, 50 kilometres upstream from Quebec, Vaudreuil planned a two-day march back to Quebec, with the forces that escaped the battlefield, overwhelm the British, and save the city. They marched only one day before word reached them that the garrison, faced with hunger and the threat of an imminent fight in which hundreds of militia and their families would be killed, had reached a negotiated surrender.

Artillery commander George Williamson was the first British soldier to march into Quebec. He found that "535 houses are burned down, besides we have greatly shattered most of the rest."

Two days after the surrender, Major George Scott returned from ravaging the south shore, with large herds of cattle and sheep and "an immense deal of plunder, such as household stuff, books, and apparel." He reported to Brigadier Robert Monckton, now in command of the British forces, that his Rangers and infantry had "burnt nine hundred and ninety eight good buildings, two sloops, two schooners, ten shallops, and several bateaus and small craft, took fifteen prisoners (six of them women and five of them children) killed five of the enemy," with three of his troops killed and five wounded.

The first Battle of the Plains of Abraham was over, but not the conquest of Canada. The French forces retreated to Montreal to fight another day.

Throughout the summer, the sisters at the Hôpital Général, beyond the range of the British south shore artillery, cared for Montcalm's sick and wounded fighters, and refugees from the city. Throughout the fall and winter, they now gave the same devoted care to the British.

With the capture of the city, Monckton, wounded, and other officers returned with the fleet to Britain. Brigadier James Murray, formerly Wolfe's fourth in command, was left in charge, to face a grim winter.

The British garrison slept in hastily repaired houses and other buildings that did little to keep out the cold. Fuel was a problem. Murray sent 800 troops to cut firewood, and rationed its use. Yet cold and scurvy took a bigger toll than all the shooting. When liquor could be found, soldiers too often drank to excess for a feeling of warmth that only hastened their death. "By April 24," writes historian D. Peter MacLeod, "2,312 members of the garrison had been hospitalized and 682 lay stacked like firewood on the frozen ground," awaiting the spring thaw and burial.

Spring would also bring the second Battle of the Plains of Abraham, aka the Battle of Sainte-Foy. At Montreal, Vaudreuil and Francois-Gaston de Lévis, now New France's military commander, assembled their forces for a campaign to retake Quebec. On April 28, 3,800 soldiers led by Lévis marched out of the woods, two kilometres southwest of the city. In a three-hour bloodbath 558 are killed, 1,610 are wound, both French and British. The outnumbered British are forced to retreat beyond the city gates. The French have won the second battle, but like the British less than eight months earlier, they have not yet captured Quebec. Both sides await the breakup of St. Lawrence ice and the arrival of ships from the across the Atlantic.

After the first Plains of Abraham Battle, Vaudreuil and Lévis sent a joint letter to Paris requesting provisions, 10,000 troops, and, perhaps most importantly, heavy artillery. With this, the French recapture of Quebec, control of Canada, and all New France, would seem almost assured.

The first battleship is sighted May 9. Is it French? Is it British? Upon that ship, and others in its wake, rest the destiny of a continent.

Quebec is rocked by an explosion of joyous shouting and the welcoming boom of blank cannon fire. The ship is the British *HMS Lowestoft.* Two more British ships arrive May 15. "I think that the colony is lost," Lévis writes. The siege is lifted. The English again hold Quebec. New France is doomed.

The French did send a token force to aid its colony: a frigate and three transport ships with 400 soldiers. None of these reached

Quebec: all were either lost at sea or captured by the British. At Montreal, on September 8, after 147 years, two months and six days of shooting at each other, the English and French finally stop fighting for control of a continent. With their force of 3,000 surrounded by 17,000 British troops, Lévis and Vaudreuil had no choice but unconditional surrender. At least in North America, the Seven Years' War was over.

Conquest of Canada won by naval battles on far side of Atlantic

It was not at the Plains of Abraham, in either the first or second battles, that the destiny of the continent was determined. It was determined two months after Wolfe's forces won the first battle and more than five months before Vaudreuil and Lévis won the second battle. It was determined by a pair of naval battles on the far side of the Atlantic. The ships that arrived in May to lift the siege of Quebec could not possibly have been French, because the French navy had been demolished.

While Wolfe was trying to figure out how to capture Quebec, in Europe, the French were planning to invade Britain. A dozen battleships of the French Mediterranean fleet were to join 21 of the Atlantic fleet, stationed at Brest, on the western tip of France and the edge of the English Channel, the staging area for the invasion. The task of Britain's Mediterranean fleet was to keep the French ships blockaded at their Toulon base. In August, the British Mediterranean fleet returned to Gibraltar for repairs and provisions. The French set sail for Brest. It took 12 days to reach the straits of Gibraltar, which they slipped past into the Atlantic under cover of night, but not undetected. The repaired and almost provisioned British fleet, 14 ships under the command of Vice-Admiral Edward Bowscawen, gave chase, overtaking seven of the French ships off the coast of Portugal. In the ensuing Battle of Lagos, the British destroyed two of the French ships and captured three others.

The French navy suffered a major blow at Lagos, but not a knockout. An invasion was still planned. The knockout punch came three months later, at the Battle of Quiberon Bay, acclaimed as "One of the most brilliant pages in naval history," by U.S. Navy Captain Alfred Thayer Mahon in his seminal book, *The Influence of Sea Power Upon History*. Britain's Atlantic fleet, under the command of Admiral Edward Hawke, joined by Bowscawen's Mediterranean fleet, attacked the French off the

Bay of Quiberon in a raging gale. The British sank six French ships, captured a seventh, and inflicted a devastating loss of 2,500 sailors, killed or drowned. Nearly all of what was left of the French navy was kept out of action for the rest of the Seven Years War by a tight British blockade. The British lost two ships and 400 sailors at Quiberon.

"The French fleet was annihilated," Mahon wrote in his gripping account of the battle. "All possibility of an invasion of England passed away with the destruction of the Brest fleet. The battle of November 20, 1759, was the Trafalgar of this war...the English fleets were now free to act against the colonies of France, and later Spain."

If there was such a thing as an English hero in the Conquest of Canada, it was Edward Hawke.

Had the French won the battles of Lagos and Quiberon Bay, annihilated the British navy, and been able to send the 10,000 requested soldiers, provisions and guns, the history of the world would likely have turned out quite differently.

The Seven Years' War that was really a nine-year war officially came to a close on February 10, 1763, with the signing of the Treaty of Paris. "No one triumphed," historian William H. Fowler wrote. "Almost nothing changed." Except in North America, where the French lost almost half a continent, the destiny of Canada was determined, the door was opened for the American Revolution, and English was entrenched as the language for most of the continent.

Readings

Fowler, William H. *Empires at War: The Seven Years' War and the Struggle for North America*. Vancouver: Douglas & McIntyre, 2005.

MacLeod, D. Peter. *Northern Armageddon: The battle of the Plains of Abraham. Eight Minutes of Gunfire that Shaped a Continent*. Vancouver: Douglas & McIntyre, 2008.

Mahon, A.T. *The Influence of Sea Power Upon History: 1660-1783*. Boston: Little, Brown, 1890. Text accessed July 21, 2012 at Project Gutenberg ebook: http://www.gutenberg.org/files/13529/13529-8.txt

National Battlefields Commission. *Battles of 1759 and 1760. The Siege of Quebec: An Episode of the Seven Years' War*. http://bataille.ccbn-nbc.gc.ca/en/siege-de-quebec/quebec-cle-de-voute.php

Parkman, Francis. *Montcalm and Wolfe*. Markham, Ontario: Penguin Books of Canada, 1984. First published in two volumes in Boston, by Little. Brown, 1884.

Wikepedia. Battle of the Plains of Abraham. http://en.wikipedia.org/wiki/Battle_of_the_Plains_of_Abraham. Accessed July 27, 2012.

William Wood. *The Plains of Abraham—September 13, 1759. The Winning of Canada. A Chronicle of Wolfe*. Toronto, 1915, Chapter VI, pp.99-139. http://faculty.marianopolis.edu/c.belanger/quebechistory/encyclopedia/WolfePlainsofAbraham.html

The incredible story of the Fraser Highlanders

Simon Fraser, Master of Lovat, chieftain of the Fraser clan, in 1757 recruited and commanded the largest regiment in WolfeÕs army, the 78th Fraser Highlanders. Twelve years earlier, he had served two years in prison for aiding the second Jacobite rebellion of 1845, which sought to depose King George II and install Charles Stewart, Bonnie Prince Charlie, on the thrones of England and an independent Scotland. His father, also named Simon Fraser, was the last man beheaded in England, in the Tower of London, for the same cause.

The senior Simon Fraser, the notorious 11th Lord Lovat, combined "all that is subtle, treacherous, and base, with all that is dangerous, desperate and remorseless," in the words of Katharine Thomson in her massive three-volume *Memoirs of the Jacobites of 1715 and 1745*.

Among his misdeeds, the 11th Lord Lovat abducted his neice, the Lady Amelia Lovat, heiress of the ninth Lord Lovat, and seized her estates. When that went awry, he raped the *widow* Lovat, and forced her into marriage. Outlawed, his estates confiscated, Lovat fled to France where he joined Jacobite supporters of the exiled King James, converted to Catholicism to gain favour with the French court, and spent 10 years in a French jail for other various misdeeds. He joined a plot to invade Britain,

in which he was to raise Highland troops for the Jacobite cause, but spilled the beans to the English. Later, when the first Jacobite uprising did occur, in 1715, he rallied his Fraser clan to fight for the English. He was rewarded with the Lord Lovat title, and the confiscated estates he had seized and lost a dozen years earlier.

In the 1745 uprising, with the promise of a Jacobite dukedom, he again switched sides, supporting the Jacobites while pretending to support King George. He rallied his clan to fight Bonnie Prince Charlie, and compelled his son to join the cause. Neither father nor son fought in the Battle of Culloden, the 45-minute bloodbath that killed the dream of an independent Scotland.

Young Simon Fraser arrived about half an hour too late to join the fight. But as many as 250 Fraser clansman died on that battlefield. In the aftermath, Lord Lovat lost his head to the axeman while the son lost the family estate, again confiscated, and spent two years in prison.

It was William Pitt, the de facto secretary of war, who took credit for hiring the Scottish rebels to fight for EnglandÕs control of North America.

"I remember how I employed the very rebels in the service and defence of their country," Pitt is quoted as stating shortly before his death. "They were reclaimed by this means; they cheerfully bled in defence of those liberties which they had attempted to overthrow but a few years before." Cheerfully or not, they certainly bled.

For young Simon Fraser, the Seven Years' War offered hope of yet once more regaining the confiscated estates. Commissioned a Lieutenant Colonel in the British army, Fraser recruited 1,529 clansmen in the Fraser Highlanders. Organized in 1857, the regiment fought the next year in the siege of Louisbourg, then in both the first and second battles of the Plains of Abraham. With the end of the Seven Year's War, the regiment was disbanded. It suffered heavy losses: of the full force of 1,529, only 887 were left.

But for his role in the 1845 rebellion, Simon would have been the 12th Lord Lovat. He remained Master of Lovat, and chieftain of the clan. With his regiment disbanded, he returned to Inverness, where he served as Member of Parliament for 21 years. He was finally rewarded the confiscated family estates, 11 years after the end of the Seven Years War, and eight years before he died.

In 1967, the 87th Fraser Highlanders were reformed as a ceremonial regiment of university and high school students who now parade daily in Montreal during the summer months, to the swirl of their pipes, the beat of their drums, and the blank firing of ancient muskets.

Readings.

78th Fraser Highlanders. Regimental History. http://www.78thfrasers.org/site/content/view/17/33/. Accessed July 18, 2012.

The Maple Leaf Forever

Too many decades ago when I first trudged to school, wearing the short knee pants that all little boys hated, *The Maple Leaf Forever* was known to every school kid in English-speaking Canada.
In days of yore
From Britain's shore.

We learned in school about the heroic victory when Wolfea defeated Montcalm on the Plains of Abraham,
And planted firm Britannia's flag
On Canada's fair domain.

Once regarded as Canada's unofficial national anthem, *The Maple Leaf* was composed in 1867, winning second place in a song-writing competition to mark Confederation. It reflected the well-established myth of the heroic Wolfe and the battle that supposedly determined the destiny of Canada, and North America. Today, it reeks with the calcified cancer of assumed superiority and class, culture, and race discrimination.

We can blame William Pitt, in his efforts to whip up public support for Britain's Seven Years' War against France and its allies, for establishing the myth, more than 250 years ago.

"Nations adore military heroes, and none more so than the English, particularly when the idol falls in battle," historian William M. Fowler Jr. writes in *Empires at War: The Seven Years' War and the Struggle for North America.*

For Pitt, the battle on the Plains of Abraham and the death of Wolfe "was the best combination a politician could hope for." In Parliament, Pitt delivered "a eulogy to Wolfe and a paean to his victory." Then, "Writers, poets, sculptors and painters went to work fashioning monuments to Wolfe in words, stone, and on canvass."

The lesson seems to be, if you want to be immortalized as a war hero, it's best to die in battle, like Nelson at Trafalgar, or Wolfe on the Plains of Abraham. Perhaps Edward Hawke would be better remembered had he died at the Battle of Quiberon Bay, where the destiny of Canada actually was determined.

Among the corpus inspired by Pitt, *The Maple Leaf Forever* was a latecomer.
The thistle, shamrock, rose entwine…

That's it. Just the Scots, Irish and English. No place at the table in very British North America for the French; nor for First Nations, Ukrainians, Chinese, Africans, or any of the vastly varied threads that are the fabric of Canada. Discrimination meant lost job and career opportunities and social ostracism for millions of non-British throughout much of the 19th and 20th centuries.

The Maple Leaf Forever was written by Alexander Muir, a veteran of Toronto's Queen's Own Rifles and the Battle of Ridgeway in the Fenian raids of 1866. He is said to have been inspired by a maple tree that stood in front of his house at Memory Lane and Laing Street in Toronto. The tree was still there in 2012.

Muir revised his song to make it more acceptable, and later version have been written to reflect the Canada of today. In Muir's first version, it was "Old England's flag," rather than Britannia's that Wolfe was said to have planted. He revised the song further with a version in which the French were represented by the Lilly. It was, however, the version embracing only the British that endured and remained popular, until slowly fading from the scene in recent decades.

New lyrics by Vladimir Radian in the winning entry of a 1997 CBC contest excised any hint of colonial imperialism, and spoke of
Our land of peace, where proudly flies
The Maple Leaf forever.

In another set of lyrics by former Canadian army chaplain D.E. Benton, our founding fathers are said to have come
In days of yore from splendid shores…
And planted firm those rights of old.

Neither of the new versions made the hit parade, while the old version was wildly popular for decades, at least among English-speaking Canadians.

Bigotry stained the song, and though its character may change, bigotry will always be with us. Yet today, bigotry in Canada is largely voiceless and powerless, swamped by our ocean of diversity. The maple leaf has long since been the symbol of conquest portrayed in Alex Muir's song. With a depth of quiet emotion, we salute it in our flag as a symbol of the world's most inclusive society, an inclusiveness that has made it one of the world's most peaceful. The song may deserve a burial, but we hail
The Maple Leaf Forever.

40,000 BC to 2012

40,000 BC *Homo sapiens* reach North America. Cross Asia-Alaska land bridge.

1,004. First European settlement in North America. Viking village at L'Anse aux Meadows occupied for four years.

1497 John Cabot visits. Sees North America, possibly Newfoundland. Claims territory for Britain.

1534 Jacques Cartier lands at Gaspé. Claims territory for France.

1541 First French colony in North America. Quebec military post Charlesbourg-Royal, established by Cartier and Sieur de Roberval.

1550 ca. Basque whalers set up North America's first industrial plant at southern tip of Labrador. Produce whale oil. Red Bay National Historic Site preserves remnants of plant, housing, graves of 160 whalers.

1558 First Newfoundland settlers.

1576-78 Martin Frobisher seeks Northwest Passage, returns to London with fool's gold.

1583 Humphrey Gilbert claims Newfoundland for Britain.

1642 Paul de Chomedey, Sieur de

C.W. Jeffreys. From the Imperial Oil Collection.

John Cabot sighting North America, 1497.

Maisonneuve, establishes Ville Marie. Now Montreal.

1649 Jesuits abandon Sainte-Marie Among the Hurons. Ontario mission burned to prevent capture by Iroquois.

1682 La Salle explores Mississippi Valley. Claims it for France, names it Louisiana.

1688 Médard Chourart des Grosseilliers and Pierre-Espirit Radisson explore Hudson Bay. Backed by London businessmen who establish Hudson's Bay Compa-

Louisbourg fortress on Cape Breton Island guarded the gateway to the St. Lawrence River entry to New France until captured and demolished by the British in 1758. Rebuilt, it is now one of Canada's most important historical sites, and a major tourist attraction.

ny [HBC] two years later. HBC obtains Ruperts Land.

1701 Iroquois sign Montreal Peace Treaty with France.

1713 Britain wins title to Hudson Bay, Newfoundland, and Acadia, except Cape Breton.

1715 France builds Fortress Louisbourg on Cape Breton.

1749 Britain establishes Halifax naval base.

1754 Nine-year French-Indian war starts.

1755 Expulsion of Acadians starts. 11,500 shipped from Maritimes to Louisiana and France over eight years

1756 Britain declares war on France. Seven-Year's war starts in North America for New World possessions.... First post office in Canada opens in Halifax.

1758 Britain captures Fortress Louisbourg. French driven from Maritimes. Louisbourg demolished, later recreated as museum.

1759 Wolfe wins Plains of Abraham Battle. But Britain hasn't yet conquered Canada.

1763 France cedes Louisiana to Spain, other New World possessions to Britain, except tiny islands St. Pierre and Miquelon.... Benjamin Franklin appointed Canada's first postmaster. Fired in 1774 for sympathizing with American colonists.... Royal Proclamation guarantees aboriginal rights in negotiations for land claims.

C.W. Jeffreys. From the Imperial Oil Collection.

James Cook and George Vancouver, first Europeans on B.C. West Coast, 1778.

1767 First public library in Canada opens at Montreal College.

1771 Samuel Hearn first European to reach Arctic coast overland.

1774 Quebec Act establishes British criminal law in Quebec. Restores French civil law, guarantees French Canadians linguistic and religious rights.

1775 Revolutionary War starts with fighting at Lexington and Concord.

1775-76 U.S. invasion of Canada defeated.

1776 First 1,124 of 40,000 United Empire Loyalists reach Halifax.

1778 First Europeans on B.C. west coast. James Cook in *HMS Resolute* and George Vancouver in *HMS Discovery* drop anchor in Nootka Sound.

1779 Fur traders merge. 16 Montreal outfits form Northwest Company to compete with HBC.

C.W. Jeffreys. From the Imperial Oil Collection.

Mackenzie's rebels march down Yonge Street on their ill-fated invasion of Toronto in 1837.

1783 American Revolutionary War ends.

1787 Frances Barkley first white woman in B.C.

1788 Britain-Canada regular sailing service starts.

1789 Alexander Mackenzie discovers Mackenzie River. Reaches river delta near Arctic Ocean.... First Ontario stagecoach service. Fort Erie to Queenston.

1790 Britain acquires 1 million acres in Ontario from Ottawa, Chippewa, Pottawatamie and Huron Indians.... Spain abandons claim to B.C. coast. Surrenders seized British ships; agrees to restitution; war averted.

1791 Canada Act creates Upper and Lower Canada.

1792-94 George Vancouver returns. Charts West Coast, Alaska to California.

1793 North America crossed. Mackenzie reaches Pacific Ocean at Bella Coola July 22. Lewis and Clark make first U.S. overland crossing 13 years later.... Upper Canada *Act Against Slavery* bans importing slaves. Full abolition in all British Empire follows in 1834... Emmanuel Allen auctioned in Canada's last slave sale.

1804 First Canadian theatre opens in Montreal.

1806 First white woman settler in Western

Canada. Marie-Anne Gaboury settles at Red River. Later becomes Louis Riel's grandmother.

1808 Simon Fraser at Pacific. Party travels Fraser River in Indian dugout canoes to site of future New Westminster.

1809 First steamboat in Canada. John Molson launches passenger ship *Accommodation* for Montreal-Quebec City service.

1811 Selkirk buys 300,000 square kilometres from HBC for Red River Settlement for displaced Scottish highlanders.

1812 Yanks invade Canada. Start two-and-a-half year war.

The Jeffrey drawings

The C.W. Jeffreys drawings on these pages are from more than one thousand historical drawings and paintings by the premier illustrator of Canadian history. Charles William Jeffreys (1869-1951) was an illustrator for the *New York Herald Tribune* and the *Toronto Star* before becoming a freelance artist and teacher after 1910. In 1952, Imperial Oil purchased Dr. Jeffreys' original drawings to retain a permanent collection, publishing a number of these in five portfolios, with accompanying historical text by Malcolm G. Parks. The drawings are "works of scholarship," the portfolio notes state. "Dr. Jeffreys was a meticulous researcher in Canadian history who took great pains to make his drawings authentic. His delineations of the costumes, furniture, weapons, and buildings of bygone generations are as true to history as the episodes many of his drawings record."

1818 Dalhousie University opens in Halifax.

1821 HBC and Northwest Company merge.

1826-32 Rideau Canal built. Ottawa to Kingston, 200 kilometres.

1828 First St. John's Rowing Regatta. North America's oldest continuous sports event.

Laura Secord, the heroine of the War of 1812, walked through enemy lines to warn about a planned American attack.

1835 Sam Slick appears in Halifax *Nova Scotian*. Thomas Chandler Haliburton's fictional Yankee clockmaker becomes one of the best-known humour figures in 19th century English literature.

1836 HBC buys Red River colony from Selkirk estate.

1837 Rebellions crushed in Upper and Lower Canada. William Lyon Mackenzie and Louis-Joseph Papineau flee to U.S.

1838 Second rebellion in Lower Canada. Robert Nelson declared president of Canadian Republic. Crushed in five days.

1839 Durham report promises responsible government. George Lambton hopes to Anglicize French Canadians.

1841 Upper and Lower Canada merged. Become Canada West and Canada East.

J.W. Bengough, Grip, August 16, 1873, McCord Museum.

A prostrate Canada lies at the foot of John A. Macdonald in this cartoon about the Pacific scandal. "Send me another $10,000" is written on Macdonald's hand. Macdonald had telegraphed CPR president Hugh Allen: "I must have another $10,000."

Canada has two sections but one legislature. First capital is Kingston.

1844 U.S. Democratic Party adopts election slogan "Fifty-four forty or fight." Seeks to extend U.S. western border to Alaska.

1846 Oregon Treaty sets Western Canada-U.S. border at 49th parallel.

1848 Last of 105 Franklin Arctic expedition survivors abandon *HMS Erebes* and *Terror*. Set out on foot for HBC post on Great Slave Lake. All perish.

1849 Amnesty Act grants immunity to exiled 1837 rebels. Mackenzie and Papineau return... Annexation Manifesto seeks Canada-U.S. union. Future Prime Minister John Abbott one of 325 prominent Montrealers who sign.

1852 10,000 homeless in Montreal fire.

1854 Free trade. Canada-U.S. Reciprocity Agreement lasts 12 years. U.S. abrogation adds impetus for British North America confederation.... Legislation abolishes seigniorial tenure in Lower Canada. 160 seigniors held land farmed by 72,000 tenants.

1856 First passenger train from Montreal to Toronto.

1858 25,000 prospectors stampede Fraser River gold rush.... Frederick Gisbourne lays first trans-Atlantic telegraph cable, Newfoundland to Ireland.

1859 American shoots stray HBC pig on San Juan Island. Britain and U.S. both claim island lying between Victoria and Seattle. Both send

McCord Musuem, 1.783

Irish radical Thomas D'Arcy McGee—journalist, poet, historian—was the most eloquent of the Fathers of Confederation. He was assassinated nine months after Confederation was proclaimed.

in troops. Kaiser Wilhelm of Germany arbitrates. Awards island to U.S.

1867 Confederation July 1. Unites Ontario, Quebec, Nova Scotia and New Brunswick in Dominion of Canada.

1868 Thomas D'Arcy McGee shot dead. First Canadian political assassination claims a Father of Confederation.

1869 Canada buys Ruperts Land from HBC: one-quarter of North America for $15 million.... Louis Riel leads Red River rebellion.

1870 Red River rebellion crushed. Riel flees to Montana.

1871 B.C. joins Canada. 6th province.

1873 Pacific scandal. John A. Macdonald government falls. Macdonald solicited election funds from Canadian PacificRailway promoter Hugh Allan. Liberals elected under Alexander Mackenzie..... Prince Edward Island joins Canada.

1876 Sitting Bull leads 2,000 Sioux Indians in flight to Canada. Escape follows massacre of George Custer and U.S. 7th Cavalry at Battle of Little Big Horn. Sioux remain under Canadian protection five years.

1877 Bell Telephone Company formed. In four months it had four subscribers.

1879 National Policy protects Canadian business. Import duties average 25%... Buffalo herds depleted. Prairie Indians starving. Mounties feed 7,000 at Fort McLeod.... Emily Howard Stowe Ontario's first licensed woman doctor.

The lumber town on Burrard Inlet known as Gas Town was incorporated as Vancouver April 2, 1886, and destoryed by fire on June 13. City hall then moved to new, air-conditioned premises.

1880 Calixa Lavallée composes *O Canada* with French lyrics.

1881 Canadian Pacific Railway incorporated. Government subsidies: $25 million cash, 25 million acres of land, 1,175 kilometres of track.

1883 Standard Time adopted. See Canadian inventions, page 36.

1884 Voyageurs sail for Khartoum. 386 Canadian volunteers lead British soldiers up Nile River to relieve besieged troops. 16 voyageurs killed in Canada's first overseas war action.

1885 Riel returns. Heads provisional government. Leads Northwest Rebellion in March. Rebellion squashed in Battle of Batoche, May 9-12... Jumbo killed. World's largest elephant hit by train.... Smallpox kills 1,391 in Montreal.... Last CPR spike driven November 2... Riel hanged November 16.

Horseless carriage arrives

Glenbow Museum NA 1777-1.

This 1903 Oldsmobile, owned by Calgary lawyer and future prime minister R.B. Bennett (shown here with his chauffeur) was the first automobile in Calgary.

George Carmack, Skookum Jim, and Tagish Charlie hit pay dirt.

1897 Victorian Order of Nurses and Women's Institute founded.... Bicycle repairman George Foote Foss builds Canada's first internal combustion motor vehicle.

1899 Canadian troops join 1899-1902 South African War.

1901 Child labour. Bureau of Labour exposes wretched conditions of child workers.... First trans-Atlantic radio message sent in Morse code from England to St. John's.

1886 Vancouver City incorporated April 2, Destroyed by fire June 13. Four buildings left standing, 50 killed.

1888 Canada's first hydroelectric power generated at Ontario paper mill.

1890 Manitoba Act abolishes separate schools for Catholics and Protestants.

1893 Montreal Athletic Association wins first Stanley Cup.

1894 First Labour Day. Inspired by Canadian journalist and labour leader Alexander Whyte Wright.

1895 Annapolis seaman Joshua Slocum first to sail solo around the world.

1896 Wilfred Laurier leads Liberals to election victory.... Yukon Gold Rush.

1905 Alberta and Saskatchewan are 8th and 9th provinces.

1906 Roald Amundsen crosses Northwest Passage. 3-year voyage.

1908 Robert Stanley Weir writes English lyrics for *O Canada*.... Lucy Maud Montgomery writes *Anne of Green Gables*.

1909 Grey Cup. Governor General Earl Grey donates cup for amateur Canadian football.... Birds tagged. Used by naturalist Jack Miner to study migration routes.

1911 Free trade signed by Canada and U.S. Subject to approval by Congress and Parliament. Congress approves but Laurier government defeated in elections. Agreement dies.... Second trans-Canada railway. Grand Trunk Pacific line reaches Prince Rupert.

1914 Canada enters First World War... *Empress of Ireland* sunk. Collision in Gulf of St. Lawrence with Norwegian ship *Storstad* costs 1,012 lives lost, 464 saved.

1915 Third trans-Canada railway. Canadian Northern line reaches Vancouver via Edmonton and Yellowhead Pass.... John McCrea writes *In Flanders Fields.*

1917 Income taxed. Temporary war measure.... Canada wins 52 square kilometres of European mud. Seven-week Passchendaele victory cost 16,000 Canadian lives.... Tragic Halifax explosion. 1,800 killed, 1,800 injured, 4,000 homeless in Canada's worst disaster.... First woman judge appointed. Helen Emma McGill joins Vancouver juvenile court.... Louise McKinney Canada's first woman legislator. Elected Alberta MLA.

1916. July 1, First of 18-day Battle of the Somme, worst in World War I: 1 million Allied and German casualties; 27,049 Canadian casualties, one-quarter of force. Of 801 in 1st Newfoundland Regiment, 733 killed or wounded.

1918 First World War ends. 628,462 served in Canada's armed forces; 60,661 killed; 173,000 wounded.... Women win vote in federal elections.... Daylight saving time starts.

1919 Troubled labour year. 22,000 workers join first Canadian general strike at Winnipeg. Two killed and 20 wounded in RNWMP attack on "Bloody Sunday." Across Canada, 139,988 workers stage 298 strikes with loss of 39 million working days during year.... First non-stop trans-Atlantic flight. British pilots Alcock and Brown fly 72 hours from St. John's to Galway, Ireland.... Railway bailout. Government establishes Canadian National Railway to take over bankrupt Canadian Northern, Grand Trunk and Grand Trunk Pacific. Government assumes big debts.

1920 Canada a founding member of League of Nations.... Royal North West Mounted Police (RNWMP) become Royal Canadian Mounted Police (RCMP).

1921 Agnes Macphail first woman MP. Only woman Member of Parliament for 14 years.... *Bluenose* schooner launched at Lunenburg.... World's largest hydroelectric plant powers up at Niagara Falls.

1922 Banting and Best discover insulin. See page 37..... Ottawa plots U.S. invasion. Secret plan in case of war.

1923 Canada dry. Prohibition almost everywhere.... Toronto Symphony Orchestra tunes up.

1924 Saskatchewan repeals prohibition.

1925 United Church of Canada begot. Presbyterians, Methodists and Congregationalists merge.... Speed skater. Toronto's 17-year-old Lela Alene Brooks sets 6 world records. Later extends that to 17.

1926 King-Byng affair. Mackenzie King Liberal government resigns June 29 over customs scandal. Governor General Byng calls on Arthur Meighen to form Conservative government July 2. Meighen government falls.

When Saskatchewan farmers, impoverished in the Great Depression, couldn't afford gasoline, they hitched up their horses to tow Bennett Buggies, named after the prime minister. Regina, 1935.

Loses confidence motion by one vote. Liberals win national elections September 14.

1927 Old Age Pensions for needy Canadians over 70... Edward Rogers invents first batteryless radio.... Hello! Are you there? Canada and Britain begin transatlantic phone service.

1928 Supreme Court says women are not persons. Can't sit in Senate.

1929 October stock market crash. Heralds 10-year Great Depression.... Women ruled persons. They can sit in Senate. Britain's Privy Council overrules Canada's Supreme Court.... U.S. Coast Guard sinks Canadian schooner *I'm Alone.* Ship in international water 320 kilometres off Louisiana. Carried 2,800 cases of liquor for prohibition-thirsty Americans. Ship's captain and crew

jailed.... World's longest suspension bridge links Windsor and Detroit.

1930 R.B. Bennett Conservative government elected.... Federal employees win 8-hour workday law... Cairine Reay Wilson first woman senator.

1932 Men work in relief camps for 20 cents a day. Single, unemployed men get food, shelter and medical care. By June, 1936, when the camps were closed, they had housed 170,000 men...... Canadian Radio Broadcasting Commission created. Later renamed CBC.... Cooperative Commonwealth Federation (CCF) organized in Calgary by socialist MPs and League for Social Reconstruction. Forerunner of New Democratic Party.

1933 23% unemployed. 1,517,531 on public relief.... Bankrupt Newfoundland reverts to colony status. Becomes British dependant.... CCF calls for nationalization of railways, banks, insurance companies and public utilities.... Communists win municipal elections in Blairmore, Alberta.

1934 World's first surviving quintuplets. Five Dionne sisters born in Callandar, Ont.... RCAF acquires first 10 fighter aircraft.

1935 On to Ottawa Trek. 1,000 jobless men hop freight cars in Vancouver. Ranks swell to 2,000. Trek ends in Regina after policeman killed in riot.... Liberals win national elections. Mackenzie King returns for second rule of 14 years.... U.S. apologizes for sinking *I'm Alone*. Pays $50,000 in compensation.

1936 Nurse Dorothea Palmer arrested for distributing birth control information. Later acquitted. Birth control literature legalized.

1937 Happy Gang sings. CBC's most popular radio musical program runs for 22 years.... Dawn to Dusk Across Canada. Inaugural flight of government's Trans-Canada Airlines (later Air Canada) launches first national airline service.... Quebec's "Padlock Law" shutters buildings suspected of spreading communism.... Mackenzie-Papineau Battalion sends 1,200 Canadian volunteers to fight fascists in Spanish civil war. Lost cause immortalized in Hemmingway novel *For Whom the Bell Tolls*.

1939 Second World War. Canada joins September 10.

1940 Quebec women win franchise. Last to vote in provincial elections.... Henry Larsen

Canadian Press 66EO94

A soldier kisses his child goodbye as he leaves to join the Second World War. October 1939

skippers RCMP patrol vessel *St. Roch* on first west-to-east crossing of Northwest Passage.... William Stephenson appointed Britain's chief espionage agent in North America. Canadian inventor and First World War fighter pilot is code named Intrepid.... Comic book imports banned.

1941 Hong Kong tragedy: 1,957 Canadian infantry fight Japanese in defence of British colony; 209 killed in battle, 204 die in war camps.... Unemployment Insurance launched.... Wartime controls freeze prices, wages, and rents.... Japanese bomb Pearl Harbour December 7. U.S. enters war.

Deborah Baic, Globe and Mail, CP Images 01591058

Leduc oil discovery, near Edmonton, propelled Canada into the ranks of major world oil producers.

1942 West coast Japanese Canadians interned. Moved to B.C. interior ghost towns. Property expropriated.... Dieppe disaster. 5,000 Canadian infantry raid French port. 907 killed, 946 captured, many wounded.... German submarine torpedoes British steamer *Nicoya* and Dutch vessel *Leo* in Gulf of St. Lawrence.... Japanese submarine lobs shells at Vancouver Island lighthouse. Misses target.... Submarine lands German spy Werner Janowski at New Carlisle, Quebec. Mounties capture him next day... Canadian RAF pilot George "Buzz" Beurling shoots down 15 enemy aircraft.... Alcan highway opens. Highway for Alaskan defence against possible Japanese invasion stretches 2,450 kilometres from Dawson Creek, B.C., to Fairbanks, Alaska.

1943 Canadian Navy assumes North-West Command. Protects North Atlantic convoys to Britain. Many casualties from German U-boat torpedo attacks.... Italy surrenders to Allies, Germans fight on. Canadian forces lead advance across Sicily and up Italy.

1944 Allies land on Normandy beaches. Five thousand Canadians killed in two-month battle to secure beachhead.

1945 War ends. Germany surrenders to Allies May 7; to Soviet Union, May 8. Japan surrenders September 2. More than 1 million Canadians served in armed forces; 44,093 killed; 54,000 wounded; 9,000 taken prisoners... Russian spy ring in Canada. Clerk Igor Gouzenko defects with documents from Russia's Ottawa embassy.... First monthly Family Allowance (aka Baby Bonus) cheques for families with children, $5 to $8 per child, depending on age. Major factor in lifting status of most Canadians from below to above defined poverty level by 1951 census.... Canada's first reactor goes nuclear. ZEEP (Zero Energy Experimental Pile) in operation at Chalk River.... Canada joins UN as a founding member.

1946 Canada's first drive-in movie theatre opens in Hamilton.... Bluenose sinks. Hits reef off Haiti.

1947 Alberta's Leduc discovery ignites Canada's oil boom.

1948 Newfoundland votes to join Canada. 10th province.... Mackenzie King retires. With 7,825 days in office, longest-serving prime minister in British Commonwealth.... PM Louis St. Laurent proposes "collective security league." Becomes North Atlantic

Tankers on the St. Lawrence Seaway, heading north on the Detroit River between Lakes Erie and St. Clair. Through rivers, lakes and canals, the Seaway stretches 3,790 kilometres from a point near Montreal to Duluth, Minnesota, on Lake Superior, conntecting the Atlantic Ocean with the heart of North America. Construction of the first locks near Montreal began in 1793. Today's Seawway, through which big ships like these tankers can pass, was not completed until 1959, a monumental engineering and construction feat.

Treaty Organization (NATO).... Barbara Ann Scott wins figure skating gold at Winter Olympics.

1949 Work starts on Toronto subway. Canada's first.... Canadian-built *Jetliner* North America's first commercial jet aircraft.... *BNA Act* amended. Enables Canada to change its constitution. Change comes 34 years later.... Fire destroys *Noronic,* largest Great Lakes passenger ship; 118 lives lost.

1950 Red River flood evacuates 100,000 Winnipegers.... Canada joins UN forces in Korean War.

1951 Old Age Pensions for all over 70, for needy aged 65... Canada to build St. Lawrence Seaway, with or without U.S.

1952 First television stations on air at Montreal and Toronto.... Atomic Energy Canada established. AECL to investigate nuclear electric power.

1953 Korean War ends. 21,940 Canadians served with UN forces. 314 killed, 1,211 wounded, 33 captured.... First Canadian indoor shopping mall opens in Toronto.

1954 World's longest pipeline delivers Alberta oil to Sarnia, Ont.... Hurricane Hazel hits Toronto. 124-km winds cause flooding, lots of damage, 83 deaths.

1956 Black Friday in Parliament. House of Commons in uproar. Government makes unprecedented use of closure to ram through bill to subsidize construction of natural gas pipeline from Alberta to

Montreal.... Lester Pearson proposes special UN Emergency Force to stop incipient Suez war. First UN Peacekeepers.

1957 Supreme Court overturns Quebec Padlock Law.... John Diefenbaker's Conservatives win national elections.... Spring Hill coalmine explosion traps 174 miners. 100 rescued over 8 days, 74 perish.... *Montreal Herald* stops publication after 146 years.... World's biggest non-nuclear explosion demolishes Ripple Rock shipping hazard off B.C. coast.

1959 First ship passes through St. Lawrence Seaway.

1960 Seven-year-old Roger Woodward survives fall over Niagara's Horseshoe Falls.

1961 Tommy Douglas first New Democratic Party leader.

1962 Saskatchewan creates medicare.... National Oil Policy rescues Alberta's oil industry. Prohibits petroleum imports west of Ottawa.... Canada's first commercial nuclear power plant fires up near Chalk River, Ontario... Trans-Canada Highway officially opened. Short Ontario section still missing.... Pamela Anne Gordon bares all. First Canadian playmate in *Playboy*.... Fog halts Grey Cup game. Resumes in Toronto next day. Winnipeg Blue Bombers beat Hamilton Tiger Cats.... CTV airs. Second national TV network.

1963 Quebec separatists turn violent. Molotov cocktails, small letter bombs, bigger bombs explode. 65- year-old night watchman killed. Queen Victoria monument in Montreal, Wolfe's statue in Quebec City,

blown up. 16 FLQ members plead guilty to terrorism.... Bush fire. Three killed, nine wounded in Kapuskasing shootout between company loggers and independent workers.

1964 Maple Leaf Flag unfurled.... SIN numbers issued. Social insurance digits for all.... Northern Dancer wins Kentucky Derby. First Canada horse to take prize.... Stock market spree. Triggered by copper-zinc-silver discovery at Timmins.

1965 Qualifying age for universal Old Age Pensions reduced from 70 to 65 years.... Auto Pact creates Canada-U.S. free trade in new cars and parts.... Newfoundland offers free tuition for first year students at St. John's Memorial University.... Final section of Trans-Canada Highway opened between Fort Frances and Atikokan, Ont.... Blackout. Millions in dark, as Ontario Hydro relay failure cuts power from southern Ontario to Florida, Atlantic coast to Chicago. Lights out for 12 hours.

1966 Colour television starts.... Defence Minister Pierre Sévigny snared in sex spy affair. Montreal prostitute Gerda Munsinger is information contact for Communist spy services.... Last Studebaker car. Automaker folds.... Canada's first topless bar opens. Vancouver's Cat's Whisker's bares half..... Nancy Greene wins gold. Rossland, B.C skier takes women's slalom at Canadian International Ski Championships.

1967 Canada celebrates Centennial Year. Montreal hosts Expo '67 World Fair. Centennial Voyageurs paddle canoes 5,283 kilometres from Rocky Mountain House to Montreal.... Charles De Gaulle cries "Vive le Quebec Libre" in Montreal. Canada is not amused.... Cunard steamships end Atlantic passenger service.

1968 Pierre Elliott Trudeau leads Liberals. Succeeds Lester Pearson as party leader and prime minister .... Political air war. Trudeau, Robert Stanfield, Tommy Douglas, Real Caouette in first national TV debate.... Trudeaumania sweeps Canada. Liberals re-elected.... Giant oil find on Arctic coast. Alaska's Prudhoe Bay is North America's biggest oil field.... Nancy Greene wins gold in women's giant slalom at Winter Olympics.

1969 Snowmobiles replace Mounties' dog teams.... Saskatchewan accepts grain for university fees.... Montreal Expos first non-American team in U.S. baseball's big leagues.... Breathalizer tests for suspected drunk drivers.... Separatist violence rocks Quebec. 27 injured in Montreal stock exchange explosion. FLQ Pierre-Paul Geoffroy pleads guilty to 31 Montreal bombings. 64 more follow. Mayor Drapeau's home bombed, but no injuries... 16-hour wildcat strike by Montreal police and firemen. 2 deaths, violence and looting.... War Measures Act invoked. 465 arrested, 18 convicted.... Montreal students protest alleged racism at Sir George Williams University. $14 million computer destroyed, data centre burned.... Canadian Coast Guard icebreaker *John A.*

Pierre Elliott Trudeau succeeded Lester Pearson as Liberal Party leader and prime minister, April 20, 1968. In elections two months later, he returned the Liberals to office on a wave of Trudeaumania and served as prime minister for 15 of the next 16 years.

Macdonald frees ice-trapped U.S. oil tanker *Manhattan*. Trial Northwest Passage run to ship Alaska's Prudhoe Bay oil. Oil later shipped instead by trans-Alaska pipeline.

1970 No more inches and miles. Canada adopts metric system.... British Trade Commissioner James Cross and Quebec Labour Minister Pierre Laporte kidnapped by FLQ terrorists. Laporte's body found in car trunk. Cross freed. Kidnappers get haven in Cuba.

1971 Four FLQ terrorists convicted of kidnapping and non-capital murder of Pierre Laporte.... Quebec plans $6 billion James Bay hydroelectric power project.... Peter Lougheed's Alberta Conservatives elected. End 36-year Social Credit rule.

1972 Canada wins hockey title with 34 second left. Paul Henderson's goal beats Russians.... Harold Ballard convicted of fraud and theft. President of Toronto Maple Leaf Gardens and Maple Leaf hockey team gets three-year jail term.... Last daily rum ration for Canada's navy sailors.

1973 Arab oil embargo. Gasoline and fuel oil shortages. Oil price jumps from $3.50 US to $11 per barrel..... Karen Kain and Frank Augustyn win first place duet ensemble at International Ballet Competition in Moscow.... Legal trouble for abortion doctor

Henry Morgantaler. Admits to 6,000 abortions but acquitted on charges. Acquittal overturned by Quebec Appeal Court. Acquittal upheld by Supreme Court. Morgantaler serves 10 of 18-month jail term. Acquitted again at a retrial in 1976. Abortion legalized in 1990.

1974 National Energy Program strains Confederation. Ottawa bites into Alberta oil revenues. Creates national oil company Petro-Canada. Oil price and exports controlled..... French language signs mandated in Quebec.

1975 Egg Marketing Agency has egg on its face. 28 million surplus "bad" eggs destroyed.... Wage and price controls imposed to curb rampant inflation.... Minimum wage for federal employees increased 20 cents to $2.60 per hour.

1976 T. Eaton Company ends publication of iconic catalogue. A century-old fixture at houses and outhouses.... Canada wins hockey's first Canada Cup. Beats Czechoslovakia in overtime.

1977 Cross Canada Via Rail. Ottawa train for national rail passenger service.... Cree and Inuit win 60% of Quebec. Big land claims settlement.... Bill 101 makes French Quebec's official language. Limits use of English.

1978 Explorers find Spanish galleon sunk off Labrador in 1525.

1979 Road to Arctic Coast opens. Dempster Highway runs 736 kilometres from Dawson to Inuvik.... Supreme Court strikes down unilingual legislatures and courts in Quebec and Manitoba.

1980 Terry Fox ends cross-Canada cancer run at Thunder Bay. Cancer spreads to lungs of one-legged runner. Dies nine months later, age 23, a national hero.... Canada rescues Americans from Iranian captivity. Ambassador Kenneth Taylor hides 6 U.S. diplomatic employees for 2 months after takeover of American embassy in Iranian revolution. They escape Tehran under cover of Canadian passports.... Quebecers reject sovereignty-association by 60-40 vote.

1981 Champagne toast for oil accord. Trudeau and Lougheed sign Alberta-Canada revenue sharing deal that calms bitter dispute. Agreement anticipates doubling of world oil prices, but price falls from $43 to $19 per barrel in seven years.... Government-owned Petro-Canada buys Belgian-controlled Petrofina Canada for record $14 billion.... Soviet Union wins Canada Cup hockey tournament.... 12.5% inflation rate is 33-year high.

Jeremy Gilbert, Wikimedia Commons

Terry Fox inspires a nation with his courage and tenacity on his cross-Canada marathon to raise funds for cancer research. Hopping on his prosthetic leg, Fox ran a full 42-kilometre marathon every day until cancer spead to his lungs, ending his journey after crossing half the continent. He is shown here in Toronto, July 12, 1980.

1982 Constitution Act replaces British North America Act. Includes Charter of Rights and Freedoms. Signed by all provinces except Quebec.... Storm sinks drill ship *Ocean Ranger* off Newfoundland. 84 killed.... Canadian economy sinks 4.8%. Biggest drop since 1933 in Great Depression. Unemployment hits 8.6%.... Europe bans imports of Canadian seal pelts.

1983 Two fisheries patrol boats sunk off Nova Scotia. 9 charged with piracy in conflict over lobster quotas.... Canadarm releases, then retrieves satellite from U.S. space shuttle.... Jeanne Sauve appointed first woman governor general.

1984 Canada wins 4 Winter Olympic medals in Sarajevo.... Wins record 44 Summer Olympic medals in Los Angeles.... 3 killed, 13 wounded in Quebec legislature. Corporal Dennis Lortie fires sub-machine gun. Wanted to destroy Parti Quebecois government.... Marc Garneau first Canadian in space.

1985 Quebec Superior Court overturns Bill 101. French-language signs violate province's Human Rights Charter.... Paraplegic Rick Hansen begins round-the-world wheelchair journey. See feature page 38.... Base metal money. Bronze $1 loonie followed by $2 toonie.... Supreme Court invalidates 95 years of Manitoba's English-only laws. Hundreds to be translated into French.... Orange light for prostitutes. Federal law prohibits soliciting in public places, impeding pedestrians or vehicular traffic.

1986 Big fossil find. Bay of Fundy collection is North America's largest.... Jetco president Keith Alexander first Canadian business executive jailed for environmental pollution.... Ontario doctors end 250-day strike over ban on extra billing.... Refugee status for 155 Sri Lanka Tamils found drifting off Newfoundland.

1987 Mulroney and provincial premiers sign Meech Lake Accord. Offers Quebec distinct society. Expanded powers for provinces. Must be ratified by Parliament and provincial legislatures.... Edmonton tornado kills 25, injures 250... Black Monday. Global stock market crash October 19 sinks Canadian shares 22.5% by month-end.... Preston Manning elected Reform Party leader.

1988 Canada-U.S. Free Trade Agreement signed.... United Church approves ordination of homosexuals.... Ottawa sells 45% ownership of Air Canada. Later sells all to Canadian investors.... Supreme Court strikes down Quebec's unilingual sign laws. Violates federal and Quebec charters. Quebec National Assembly invokes constitutional "notwithstanding clause" to maintain sign laws.

1989 Audrey McLaughlin elected NDP leader. First Canadian woman to lead a national political party.... 14 women killed, 9 wounded in University of Montreal shoot-

First same-sex marriage, Montreal, April 1, 2004. First same-sex divorce, Toronto, September 14.

ing rampage. Shooter Marc Lepine commits suicide. Says feminists spoiled his life.

1990 Nova Scotia Micmac Indian Donald Marshall Jr. found wrongfully convicted of 1971 murder. Served 11 years in jail.... Four million tires burn for 17 days. Spew toxic smoke at Ontario tire dump. 4,000 residents evacuated.... Mohawk gambling turns violent. Armed warriors overrun blockades set up by opponents of commercial gambling on Quebec's Akwesasne reserve. 500 residents flee violence on reserve.... Elijah Harper kills Meech Lake Accord. Cree MLA refuses unanimous consent to introduce Accord in Manitoba legislature. Says it fails to recognize aboriginal rights.... Bloc Quebecois political party formed by Liberal and Conservative MPs.

1991 Goods and Services taxed.

1992 Charlottetown Accord defeated in Quebec referendum. Successor to failed Meech Lake Accord. Second attempt to win Quebec's accession to Constitution.... Toronto Blue Jays win baseball World Series. Win again in 1993.

1993 Atlantic cod fishery shut down to rebuild depleted stock.... Kim Campbell succeeds PM Brian Mulroney. Canada's first woman prime minister. PC's reduced to 2 seats in following elections. Jean Chretien returns Liberals to office.

1994 800,000 killed in Rwanda genocide. UN fails to heed General Dellaire's request for 5,000 troops to bolster 420-man police keeping force.... North American Free Trade Agreement inked. Embraces Canada, United States and Mexico. Replaces Canada-U.S. Free Trade.... Navy seizes Spanish trawler. Broke Grand Banks fishing ban. Dubbed Turbot War.

1995 Quebec separation defeated again. Referendum rejected 50.6% to 49.4%... Medicine Hat flood evacuates 50,000... Gun control law prohibits most handguns. Rifles must be registered.... Guy Paul Morin's murder conviction overturned. Served 11 years in jail.... Woman top cop. Calgary's Christine Silverberg Canada's first female police chief.... Paul Bernardo gets life sentence. No parole. Convicted of kidnap, rape and murder of Leslie Mahaffy, Kristin French, and Tammy Lyn Homolka. Wife and murder partner Karla Homolka testified against him. Gets 12-year jail term.... Canadian National Railways privatized.... Canada sends 1,000 peacekeepers to Bosnia.

1996 Quebec floods kill 10. Demolish 2,600 homes in Saguenay District.... Canada organizes Arctic Council. Embraces 10 circumpolar countries.... Former B.C. Premier Bill Bennett convicted of insider trading.

1997 80,000 evacuated in Manitoba and North Dakota floods. Damage estimated at $35 US billion.... Canada signs UN Kyoto Protocol. Ratified by Parliament 5 years later. Pledge to cut greenhouse gas emissions 6% below 1990 level by 2012 is far from achieved.... Oil flows from Hibernia. Canada's first major offshore oil field is 315 kilometres east-southeast of St. John's.

1998 Millions freeze in dark in Great Ice Storm. Freezing rain knocks out power for up to 30 days. Blackout stretches from southeastern Ontario to Nova Scotia and New England. Storm kills 35, injures 945.

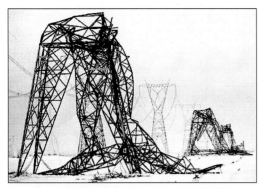

Freezing rain toppled power lines in 1998 storm, leaving millions of people from southeastern Ontario to New England without power for up to 30 days.

Up to $7 billion in damages.... Dollar worth $0.64 US. Record low.... 20,000 on Parliament Hill protest long gun registration.

1999 Nunavut now Canada's third territory. Carved from 60% of Northwest Territories. One-fifth of Canada is home for 27,000 people.... RCAF fighter jets join NATO bombing raids to force Serbian troops out of Kosovo.... T. Eaton Company files for bankruptcy.

2000 Reform Party renamed Canadian Alliance. Wins 66 seats in national elections. Becomes official opposition. Progressive Conservative Party 5th with 12 seats.

2001 Canada hosts 35,000 stranded Americans. Terrorist attacks on New York and Washington divert 224 U.S. planes to Canada.... Canada first to legalize medical marijuana.

2002 Canadian troops join U.S.-led forces in Afghanistan war on terrorists.... Canada commits $10 billion over 10 years to combat spread of weapons of mass destruction....

Canada wins Olympic gold for men's and women's hockey teams at Salt Lake City.... Stephen Harper elected Canadian Alliance leader.

2003 Alliance and Progressive Conservative parties merge. Form Conservative Party. No more "Progressive Conservative" oxymoron.... SARS epidemic kills 44 in Toronto. Poor hospital infection-control procedures blamed for Severe Acute Respiratory Syndrome.

2004 Harper elected Conservative leader March 28. Conservatives win 99 seats in June 28 elections..... Auditor General uncovers sponsorship scandal. No work performed for $15 million federal advertising contract in Quebec. Most of the money kicked back to Liberal Party.... Supreme Court upholds child spanking "within limits.".... World Health Organization endorses Canadian plan to deal with avian flu epidemic. 19 million B.C. poultry slaughtered.... First same-sex marriages. Michael Hendricks and René Lebouf wed in Montreal April 1. First same-sex divorce granted September 14 to Toronto lesbian couple.... Nelson, B.C. rejects planned monument to American draft dodgers.

2005 Civil Marriage Act legalizes same-sex marriage across Canada.... Four Mounties shot dead in drug raid on Meyerthorpe, Alta. farm.... CBC journalist Michaëlle Jean appointed Governor General.... First ever Commons tie-breaking vote. Speaker Peter Millikin's vote sustains Paul Martin's minority Liberal government.... No-confidence motion defeats government November 28... Natalie Glebova wins Miss Universe title. Russian-born Canadian classical pianist.... Ian and Sylvia's *Four Strong Winds* named Canada's greatest song.

2006 Canada and Russia veto UN Draft Rights of Indigenous People.... Harper Conservatives elected minority government.... Terrorist plot uncovered. Ontario youths planned to behead Harper, kidnap MPs, blowup Parliamentary buildings and military installations.... Ontario blackout. Thunderstorms, tornadoes leave 200,000 without power for up to one week.... Elizabeth May elected Green Party leader.

2007 Newspaper publisher Conrad Black convicted of three charges of fraud and one of obstructing justice.... Appeal Court overturns Steven Truscott 1959 murder conviction of Lynne Harper.

2008 Foreign Affairs Minister Maxime Bernier leaves confidential NATO documents in home of girl friend, who is linked to Hells Angels.... Harper calls 2-month Parliamentary recess. Averts defeat on non-confidence motion. Kills planned Liberal-NDP coalition government.

2009 Ghostnet uncovered. University of Toronto researchers discover Chinese cyber spying. Hackers infiltrated top political, economic and media computer resources in more than 100 countries.

2010 Canada wins record medals at 21st Winter Olympics: 14 gold, 7 silver and 5 bronze at Vancouver and Whistler. Canadian men's and women's hockey teams both win gold, defeating U.S. teams.... Warmest driest winter. Average 2009-10 winter 4^0 C. above normal.... Accusations of political payola haunt Treasury Board President Tony Clement.... University of Waterloo president David Johnston appointed Governor General.... Judge rules brothels and streetwalking legal.

2011 Conservative government in contempt of Parliament. Failed to provide cost information about planned purchase of fighter jets and construction of new jails. Government falls on non-confidence motion. Returned to power with majority in national elections.... Winter 2010-2011 is 2.5^0 above normal.

2012. *Ending the Long-Gun Registry Act* kills 15-year law requiring ownership registration of non-restricted firearams; records to be destroyed. Quebec Superior Court imposes injunction; says registry an effective and economical crime prevention tool... Alison Redford extends 25-year Alberta rule of Progressive Conservatives. Election day polls forecast majority Wildrose Party government, but PC's win 61 seats to 17 for Wildrose.... September 19. 14-year-old Annaleise Carr is youngest to swim Lake Ontario, landing at Mississauga where Marilyn Bell made the first crossing in 1954 at age 16 (page 35). Against an adverse storm, Carr swam the 52.5-km "traditional Marilyn Bell route;" Bell swam a 54-km route. Carr's swim raised an initial $90,000 for Camp Trillium, a camp for children with cancer.

Debtors die in squalor of world's worst jails

Debtors in Upper Canada languished and died in the stink, starvation and suffocation of what was said to be the world's worst jails in the early nineteenth century. Women were not sentenced to debtors' jail, but if your family was destitute, they joined you. Men, women and children, crowded the jails. If death seemed preferable, it was hastened by lack of sanitation and ventilation, overcrowding, near starvation rations of sometimes-rotten food, illness, and disease. At Niagara, a man confined to a windowless, unventilated prison cell, eight-foot-square, died of suffocation when the summer temperature hit 105 Fahrenheit (41 Celsius).

Upper Canada's jails might have been the world's worst, but they were not a great deal better anywhere in Canada, nor in Britain. Charles Dickens, whose father died in one, described life in Britain's debtor jails in his novel *Little Dorrit*. Little Dorrit was born, raised, cared for her father, married, and spent her entire life in jail.

Canadian editors courageous enough to defy the authorities assailed jail conditions and the senseless imprisonment of debtors, which helped neither debtors nor creditors.

When a prisoner died, a jury ruled that it was a case of "Death by the visitation of God."

Incubators of crime

Perhaps the first Canadian editor to tackle the issue was Henry Chubb, whose *New Brunswick Courier* on February 2, 1822 did so by reprinting *On the Imprisonment of Debtors,* by Samuel Johnson, the eighteenth century lexicographer, author and critic. It dealt with the issue in England—where 20,000 debtors out of a population of six million lingered in jail—but drew attention to the issue in Britain's North American colonies.

"When twenty thousand reasonable beings are heard all groaning in unnecessary misery by.... the mistake or negligence of policy, who can forbear to pity and lament, to wonder and abhor," Johnson wrote.

Johnson estimated the public cost of imprisoned debtors at £300,000 pounds a year, "in ten years to more than a sixth part of our circulating coin."

He saw the debtor-filled jails as incubators of spiralling crime and evil. "The misery of goals is not half their evil: they are filled with every corruption which poverty and wickedness can generate between them; with all the shameless and profligate enormities that can be produced by the impudence of ignominy, the rage of want, and the malignity of despair."

WORLD'S WORST JAILS

Reform editor Francis Collins was in York jail barely starting a prison term for libel against the authorities and members of the notorious Family Compact when he wrote this account of Canada's treatment of insolvent debtors, published in the Canadian Freeman, *December 11, 1828.*

Of all the countries on earth, we believe there is none in which insolvent debtors are so barbarously treated as in Canada—the laws respecting them are a disgrace to British Jurisprudence—sufficient to put humanity to the blush— and call aloud for wholesale amendment.

In Canada, an unfortunate man who incurs a debt of a few dollars, without the means of liquidating it, is liable to be incarcerated, at the discretion of a merciless creditor, during the rest of his natural life! At home [i.e., England], no ordinary debt (except a fraud be proved) can deprive a man of his liberty longer than two or three months—in the U. States the term is still shorter, and they are threatening to abolish the practice altogether. In Canada, they are cooped up in a filthy apartment, for life, without bed, bedding, victuals, or any other thing to support nature, save the bare walls that surround them.

Is this just? Is it honest? Is it Christian? Can Heathen persecution exceed it?

We have at the moment above our heads *twelve* able-bodied stout men, committed to this goal for paltry debts, endeavouring to pass away dull time in playing marbles, like children—without even the consoling ray of hope ourselves enjoy, that at a given period, however distant, an end will be put to their sufferings.

DEATH BY SUFFOCATION

York was not the only jail in Upper Canada where conditions were miserable. An inquest jury in Niagara in the summer of 1830 blamed conditions in the jail there on the death of one Isaac Hoff.

Hoff had been convicted of assault. "A highly respectable and intelligent jury," according to a local paper, *Spirit of the Times,* found that he "came by his death by suffocation, in consequence of being confined by the Magistrates in a cell not sufficiently ventilated." Hoff had been confined to a jail "about eight feet square, without the light of Heaven," at a time when the ambient temperature in the shade rose to 105 Fahrenheit. In York, the *Canadian Freeman* claimed the jury would have been justified

Painting by John G. Howard, Archives of Ontario.

York (Toronto) jail, where a legislative committee in 1830 found a debtor with his wife and five children among the prisoners.

in charging the magistrates with murder. The reports were cited in Montreal's *Vindicator,* July 7, 1830.

In Brockville, when convicted murderer Henry Hamilton died in his prison cell three weeks before he was due to be hanged, an inquest jury concluded that it was a case of "Death by the visitation of God," the *Upper Canada Gazette* reported on September 9, 1825.

And the *Bathurst Examiner*, in October 1829, facetiously noted that "There is not one prisoner now confined to the Jail in the Bathurst District, and the mice are starving."

STARVATION, STINK, SQUALOR

A report of a committee of the Upper Canada House of Assembly, signed by William Lyon Mackenzie as chairman, describes a living hell in the jail at York. Excerpts from the Colonial Advocate, *February 25, 1830.*

In the cells below the ground floor, your committee found three female lunatics confined. They are lodged in locked up cribs, on straw, two in one crib, and the other by herself. A gentleman confined for debt complained that the smell from the dungeon in which these poor lunatics are confined, which below the room was almost insupportable, and that their incessant howlings and groans were annoying in the extreme. Their confinement is severe beyond that of the most hardened criminal.

Your Committee found twenty five persons in this prison; twelve criminals on the ground floor, one criminal sick upstairs, one vagrant, three lunatics above mentioned, and nine debtors.

Thomas McMahon, a criminal, complained that he had only a jail allowance of three half pence worth, one pound of bread, and water; that soap, sufficient to keep the prisoners clean, was not given; that some of the prisoners are several weeks together, without changes of linen; that he had enough bed clothes, but that they had not been washed, he believed, for six or eight months. The smell of his dungeon was very noisome.

All the other prisoners in this ward complain of the scantiness of the jail allowance, only three half pence worth of bread per diem. Your Committee think that although a place of imprisonment is not intended to be a place of comfort, it should not be a place of starvation. This allowance is too small; it is less, your Committee understands, than the allowance in other Districts, and is especially hard towards those who have not friends to help them. The request of the prisoners is six pence a day, or its value in bread.

The cell of James McMahon, and that of John Wilson, stink so as scarcely to be fit to breathe in. The jail itself is ill constructed; and the jail privy being stopped up adds to the unwholesomeness of the atmosphere, in a degree, that even in winter, is almost intolerable. The water closets ought to be taken away, and proper substitutes provided; the chloride of lime, or some other salt, ought to be used from time to time, to purify the apartments, and such other means used as would render a residence within these walls less grievous.

The debtors are, with one exception, all on the upper floor, apart from the other prisoners. These are allowed no support from their creditors, and some of them say they are entirely without the means of subsistence. James Colquhoun is in jail for a debt of three pounds; the creditor has forgiven the debt, but the lawyer has not thought proper to forgive his fees. Colquhoun subsists entirely on the humanity of the jailer and other debtors. One Murphy told your Committee that he had nothing to eat and that both Colquhoun and himself had been for days together, without tasting a morsel.

One debtor is in jail, together with his wife, and a family of five children.

ABOLITION

Imprisonment for debt was abolished throughout Canada at different times; in Quebec in 1849, New Brunswick in 1874, and in Ontario, one of the last, at the end of the nineteenth century. Some debtors, however, are still sent to prison, but not because of their debts. Those found guilty and sentenced for fraud are frequently also debtors. And "deadbeat dads," who fail to comply with court orders for family support payments, can be jailed

Public Archives Canada A054666

Spectators peered over the prison walls to see the hanging of Stanislaus Lacroix at Hull, Quebec, in 1902.

Public hangings drew big crowds of avid spectators

Public hangings were popular spectacles in the nineteenth and early twentieth centuries. Crowds jammed public squares and prison courtyards to see murderers, thieves and rebels dangling from the end of a rope. When public hangings were abolished, avid spectators crowded rooftops, climbed telephone poles and attempted to batter down prison gates to see people killed.

Legislation banning public hangings came into effect on January 1, 1870, but it wasn't always effective. The law was sometimes bent when scaffolds were built higher than prison walls to allow public viewing. Spectators climbed telephone poles and sat on rooftops to witness the hanging of Stanislaus Lacroix in 1902, as seen in the accompany photo. When Timothy Candy was hanged in Montreal in 1910 for shooting and killing two policemen, dozens of spectators witnessed the event in similar fashion.

A sheriff or prison warden had the authority to invite spectators and newspaper reporters to hangings, and the numbers of guests sometimes made the event quite public, in fact if not in name.

Mob riots to see double hanging

The most notorious and widely- viewed of Canada's nonpublic hangings was the double hanging of Cordelia Viau, a church organist, and her lover, farm worker Sam Parslow, at the village of St. Scholastique, 50 kilometres north of Montreal, at 8 a.m. on Friday, March 10, 1899. They had been found guilty of a particularly gruesome murder of Cordelia's husband, Isidore Poirier, a carpenter.

Not less than two hundred invited people crowded the jail yard to witness the hanging, although one newspaper account claimed, "It is certain that there were six hundred of them." Outside the prison walls, an estimated two thousand rioters tried to breakdown the prison gate to gain entrance. Police fired revolvers in the air to warn them back.

The event made newspaper front pages across Canada and the United States, and much later became the basis for a French language book and a movie. American Sunday newspapers lapped up the story in widely syndicated sensational accounts, such as that in the Syracuse *Sunday Herald,* March 12, 1899.

At "half a minute past eight" a procession including the prisoners, the sheriff, two priests and the police escort emerged from the jail and proceeded to the scaffold and the awaiting hangman," the *Herald* reported. "It was but three and one-half minutes

later when the trap had been sprung and all was over."

But not quite. Immediately following the drop, "A wild rush was made for the scaffold, and in a twinkling the black cloth was torn away and the bodies exposed to view." "Cordelia Viau's pulse stopped in six and one-half minutes;" Parslow's "in twelve and a half minutes."

The book about the event, *Le lampe dans fenêtre,* by Pauline Cadieux and the 1980 film, *Cordélia,* portrays the hanged woman in a sympathetic light and questions whether she was in fact guilty.

The last known public hanging in Canada, at least the last officially authorized as such, was the hanging of Nicholas Melady at Goderich, Ontario, for the murder of his father and stepmother on December 7, 1869. Although no longer officially conducted in public, convicted murderers continued to be hanged in Canada for at least another 93 three years.

Eager ladies press for close-up look

Women as well as men flocked to watch public hangings in the nineteenth and early twentieth centuries. That much is clear from photos and drawings of crowds of spectators, although the men seem to somewhat outnumber the women. None appeared more fascinated by the gruesome sight of death than the eager women who pressed in close for a detailed look at the death features of a pair of men hanged in Cayuga, Ontario. The women were admonished by the Brantford

Expositor, *in this item republished in the* Toronto Leader, *May 26, 1855.*

Stand back there boys, and give the ladies a chance to see. Where and by whom, think you, was this gallant, this considerate request made? Was it at a Charitable Show Bazaar or Floral Exhibition? Not a bit of it. T'was when Blowes and King, from the scaffold in the grove at Cayuga, dropped from time into eternity. When the murderer's cap that covered the Blowes' face was torn from crown to chin, exhibiting in all its horrible distortion the countenance of a strangled human being.

"Stand back and give the ladies a chance to see," shouted a constable from the scaffold, and he waved his stick, his badge of office, to render more expressive the words. "Make way for the ladies."

The crowd divided and the ladies, with eager eyes and hasty steps, approached the dead men. The hangman, black and ugly, steeled in heart and damnable as his vocation is, shuddered at the spectacle and drew himself away in loathing.

The ladies looked upon the bodies of the murderers, gazed upon the big veins well nigh bursting with blood, the tense muscles of the face, the protruding eyes staring in all their horror out beyond the lids. The ladies feasted on the loathsome sight, and departed gratified. The ladies will speak of what they saw at Cayuga for many a day to come, and think nothing in their conduct unwomanly, bad, unfeeling or degrading.

Had we many of such mothers, daughters, sisters, we had many Kings and Blowes. Shame upon them. Thanks be to God, in Haldimand [county] there are few

like them, though the few must make the many blush with shame. They have cast a stigma on the very name of woman; and every woman of feeling, tenderness, delicacy and refinement, cannot but mourn over their sisters' insensibility and shamelessness.

By all means advocate the policy of capital punishment. The Cayuga exhibition illustrates its wisdom, and establishes its effect.

Debtors keep cow, sheep, hog, firewood

A cow, three sheep, a hog, a stove and a cord of firewood were to be exempt from the goods that a creditor could seize from a debtor, under provisions of a bill before the Lower Canada House of Assembly. From debate in the Assembly, as reported in the Montreal Vindicator, *February 2, 1831.*

Mr. Lee looked upon this measure as one that would greatly tend to reduce the evils of mendacity, for which every means, direct and indirect, ought to be employed. He was mortified to find that the sordid spirit of mercantile avidity so strenuously opposed it… [All would benefit from the Bill], even the dealer who speculates upon the distress of his neighbours. He will learn more caution in giving credit.

This measure will greatly reduce the evils of poverty… But the greatest good would arise from it to wives and families of poor debtors, who often, by the profligacy and vices of their husbands, encouraged and promoted by the sordid expectations of gain of the shopkeepers they deal with, are reduced to the utmost distress and destitution, and see their last little property sold for next to nothing.

They will now at all events be able, with a cow and stove, to feed and warm their poor children; and their spirit of industry will be revived to retrieve the affairs of the little family. The women, the wives and mothers, were the most to be considered in the protection that was thus to be given; and he spoke not only in allusion to the families of Canadians, but the families of the Scotch and Irish settlers, who form so valuable a portion of our population.

Insolvent and bankrupt persons (the two are legally different) today still have some protection against creditor seizure of some assets or property, but the complex laws vary in each province.

Hanging for theft of horse or turnips among 230 capital crimes

For some two centuries, the death penalty hung over the parts of North America that eventually became Canada, before it was abolished—for all but military crimes.

Under British law, there were some 230 crimes that carried the death penalty, early in the nineteenth century. You could be hanged for stealing a horse or turnips, or for being found disguised in the forest.

Attitudes about such legal severity seemed mixed. When a convicted horse thief and two burglars were hanged in Montreal, it was seen by the *Upper Canada Gazette* in York as fitting, and "justice is satisfied."

"The fate of these culprits will, we trust, prove a salutary lesson to those whom they have left behind, whose moral and religious conduct require a warning for the amendment of their lives," said the *Upper Canada Gazette,* November 6, 1823.

Authorities in Lower Canada seemed more lenient, with perverse effect. The authorities, said a grand jury, were "Increasingly reluctant" to impose such harsh laws. "The parties offended refuse to prosecute; petty jurors are unwilling to convict; and his Majesty's Representative is, in almost every capital case, petitioned by numbers to exercise the Royal prerogative of mercy."

The result was that "Impunity is enjoyed by the most atrocious and hardened offenders," the report, published in the *Montreal Herald* and reprinted in the Kingston *Chronicle,* September 29, 1826, declared. Some were said to have been convicted of capital crimes as many as six times, and pardoned each time. The jurors claimed that the "public mind is ripe" for more humane laws that could afford "convicts some chance and encouragement to redeem their character" and "become useful members of society."

It took 30 years, but reform did come in 1859, when the number of crimes subject to the death penalty was reduced to 10 under the Constituted Statues of Canada (then comprising Lower and Upper Canada). It was now confined to "murder, rape, treason, administering poison or wounding with the attempt to commit murder, unlawfully abusing a girl under ten, buggery with man or beast, robbery with wounding, burglary with assault, arson, casting away a ship and exhibiting a false signal endangering a ship."

In 1865, capital punishment was again limited, to murder, treason and rape.

The abolition campaign

The most determined effort to fully abolish the death penalty was launched in Parliament in 1914 by Robert Bickerdike (1843-1928), businessman, Liberal politician, and social reformer.

Bickerdike left the family farm in Beauharnois county, Quebec, at age 17 to learn the butcher trade in Montreal, soon establishing

Wikipedia.org. Encyclopedia Canadian Biography, Montreal, 1904-07.

Robert Bickerdike led crusade to abolish capital punishment.

a meat packing business, later expanding into insurance, finance and shipping. As a politician, he was a champion of minority rights—Jews in particular—an early advocate of women's suffrage, and bent on an almost lifelong mission to abolish the death penalty.

On February 5, the House of Commons spent "practically all day" debating Bickerdike's private member's bill to abolish the death penalty. "The House seemed to be about evenly divided" on the issue, according to the *Toronto Star.*

Opponents of the bill argued that the death penalty was needed to deter murder. Frank Oliver, publisher of the Edmonton *Bulletin* and former interior minister in the Laurier government, cited Judge Matthew Bigbie as evidence. A London lawyer sent in 1858 to keep law and order in the gold mining camps of British Columbia, Bigbie is reputed to have claimed, "Boys, if there is shooting, there will be hanging." "There was shooting, and there was hanging after that," Oliver told the House. "Then there was no more shooting."

It was also claimed that capital punishment is "less degrading to society than the incarceration for life of a helpless prisoner." One MP told the House: "If the choice were put before the convicts in Kingston Penitentiary, I am not sure that the majority… would not say, bring on the rope."

Capital punishment, argued the bill's supporters, is morally wrong, opposed by religious strictures, and does not deter murder or crime.

"We cannot atone for the loss of life by taking another life," said Bickerdike. "No man who believes in his Creator dare vote against a bill to abolish legalized murder."

As it turned out, no MP had to vote that year against abolishing the death penalty. Justice Minister and Attorney General Charles Doherty, who opposed the bill, adjourned the long debate at 10:30 in the evening, and it did not come up again until the following year, when it fared no better.

Bickerdike introduced another ill-fated bill to abolish capital punishment in 1916.

Sitting on the editorial fence

When it came to taking a stand for or against capital punishment, newspapers generally appeared to be sitting on the editorial fence, apparently still undecided about the issue, as were most Canadians. Typical was the stand of the *Toronto Star* (February 9, 1920), which argued only that "There should be one law for all. There is not now one law for all… The procedure by which a popular criminal escapes the gallows is not unlike that by which a popular fellow gets a comfortable office under government."

Arguments for and against the death penalty erupted sporadically on newspaper pages during the next few decades. In the Toronto *Globe,* a clergyman implied a defence of capital punishment in 1920 while another clergyman opposed it the following year.

On January 17, 1920, in his weekly "Sunday School Lesson" *Globe* columnist, Rev. G.C. Pidgeon implied that a very vengeful God was on the side of swift and decisive retribution. "God has always punished with exceptional severity sins of presumption," Pidgeon wrote. When Arron's two intoxicated sons, Nadab and Abihu, "offered fire on God's alter, they were smitten with instant death." When army sentinels fall asleep on the job, according to Pidgeon, it is "a capital offence for which men have deserved to die."

On August 1, 1921, Rev. A. Mason hoped that Canadians would follow the example of the Swedish people who, he said, "rose up in their might and abolished the death penalty." This was apparently accomplished in spite of Sweden's executioner who, Mason noted, "has an axe to grind."

Bikerrdike did not live long enough to see the triumph of his cause. The last executions in Canada came more than half a century after he first urged abolition of the hangman's rope in Parliament.

The last two were Ronald Turpin and Arthur Lucas, hanged at the Don Jail in Toronto on December 11, 1962. Turpin had robbed the Red Rooster restaurant of $632.84 and was driving from the scene when he was pulled over by a police officer for a broken taillight. He shot and killed the policeman. Lucas, an American, had left his Detroit home for a trip to Toronto where he killed a witness in the trial of a Michigan drug lord, and also the witness' girlfriend.

In 1967 Parliament passed a government bill to abolish capital punishment and impose life imprisonment for all murders, for a five-year trial, by a vote of 105 to 70. Excluded from the abolition were murders of on-duty police officers or prison guards. In 1973 MPs sustained the five-year trial by a margin of 13 votes. Three years later, they voted to abolish all forms of capital punishment—except under the Defence Act—by a scant margin of six votes. A bill to restore the death penalty was more decisively defeated in 1987 by a vote of 148 to 127. Under the Defence Act, however, the death penalty can still be imposed on military personnel for cowardice, desertion, unlawful surrender, and spying for the enemy.

A destitute Irish woman dies foresaken on a Quebec wharf

This is the story of a poor Irish woman who was trundled by her husband through the streets of Quebec City in a vain search for shelter, only to die on the planks of a wharf. The desolate fate of the unknown Irish woman was a harbinger of much worse to come during the next quarter century. The story is told in this letter in the Montreal Gazette, August 3, 1822, reprinted from the *Quebec Mercury.*

Sir,—Through the medium of your paper I wish to draw the attention of the magistrates, to what occurred on Sunday morning at Jones's wharf; a circumstance in its nature disgraceful to a civilized country, and highly dangerous to the public.

A vessel* from Ireland, with settlers, is at this wharf, amongst which it seems there has been great sickness and many deaths; the writer of this, passing, saw a crowd, and on advancing to learn the reason, perceived a poor woman, then actually dying where she had been all night and the greater part of the day before. The circumstance of the case on inquiry, proved that a lodging had been procured for this poor creature, but on bringing her to it, admittance was refused, she was drawn through St. Rock suburbs and Champlain street, and tho' the poor man, her husband, offered probably his all, a guinea, to have her taken into some house, a lodging could not be obtained.

On his return to the vessel, he then met with a still greater disappointment, for the captain refused to take her on board; he was therefore obliged to lay her on the wharf, where I have since learned, *she died.*

One of the seamen informed me, that some of the hands had taken the fever and were now ill on board; that, in consequence, himself and the remainder had left the vessel, as she was full of sick.

I wish not, Mr. Editor, to blame any one; but is there not a Health Officer, paid for attending on vessels and persons of the above description; therefore, why is disease, and that of a most dangerous kind, allowed to be introduced among us?

I am told a fever of a very alarming nature rages in Ireland; and I trust that a little more attention will be paid to vessels arriving from thence. *AN INHABITANT.*
*The Schooner William.

Cholera enters North America through port of Quebec

Immigration ships from Britain—also known as coffin ships—brought cholera to North America, as depicted in this New York Punch *drawing, July 18, 1883.*

Some 52,000 immigrants, mostly destitute Irish, arrived at Quebec in 1832, carrying with them the cholera pandemic to first reach North America. An estimated 9,000 people died of cholera in Lower and Upper Canada in the first pandemic. By 1872, an estimated 20,000 had died. The disease could have been stopped in its tracks if medical science had then known that it was spread in cholera-contaminated water that people drank, or more rarely, in food they ate. Clean, safe drinking water would have stopped the disease. But it was thought that cholera was spread in the polluted air of early nineteenth century towns. Thus cannons shot blank charges skyward and great fires of tar and rosins were lit in efforts to clean the air.

On August 28, 1817, the government of Bengal, India, reported the outbreak of a cholera epidemic at its capital, Jessor. Ten thousand people perished within a few weeks. Twenty-four years and ten months later it would reach North America, landing at the port of Quebec, and from there it spread west as far as Niagara, and south into the United States.

From Jessor, the cholera crawled across Asia and China, reaching Russia in the summer of 1831. With reports from British papers that were two months old, Canadian newspapers in late 1831 began reporting cholera's march across Europe. At St. Petersburg, there were 4,694 cholera deaths within four months; at Moscow, 2,908 deaths within six weeks, according to Montreal's *Canadian Courant.*

Cholera reached Britain, at Sunderland, on October 26, causing "great alarm… throughout England," the *Courant* reported on January 4, 1832. The Montreal *Vindicator,* March 23, said 44 had been killed in Scotland by January 24. The *Niagara Gleaner,* March 31, said the cholera victims in Edinburgh and Glasgow were mostly from "the lowest ranks of life." Police were stationed at all the entrances to Edinburgh to "prevent the admission of beggars and other characters," while within the city, orders had been issued "for the arrest of all beggars and vagrants," who were to be temporarily confined. A month later, April 29, a *Gleaner* report estimated the death toll in Paris at 20,000 to 30,000. "By orders of the Government, the funerals are conducted by night, and trenches, instead of graves, are dug for the reception of bodies, which were brought in cartloads" by army horses. "Riots and insurrections are occurring almost every day… multitudes are thrown out of employment."

The newspaper reports were warning flags, raising fears about the record number of immigrants from Britain and Ireland that were expected to start arriving in Canada by late spring, and the danger that cholera could come with them.

Preparing for the bug

It was from the Canadian newspapers that Matthew Whitworth-Aylmer, fifth Baron Aylmer, governor general of both Lower and Upper Canada, learned that cholera had reached Britain. The ships that had carried Canadian timber to Britain in their holds, would soon be returning with immigrants crammed in their holds, more immigrants sandwiched between decks in steerage class, and a few in the relative comfort of cabins above deck. Aylmer called on his executive council to prepare for a cholera invasion.

Britain had prepared for a cholera invasion by establishing local boards of health. The British plans had been sent to officials in the Empire's far-flung colonies. Canada would follow the British pattern. The House of Assembly on February 25 passed an Act to establish a quarantine station at Grosse Île (Grosse Isle in the newspapers of the time), 50 kilometres downstream from Quebec on the St. Lawrence, and local health boards at Quebec and Montreal, with provision for boards at other centres as needed. The Act provided £10,000 to fund the health boards and the quarantine station. In March, another controversial act imposed a head tax of

> **Great effort was made to cleanse the air with big bonfires and cannon firing, not knowing cholera was carried in polluted water, not the foul air.**

five shillings per immigrant, to be paid by ships' captains, with the money used to assist sick and indigent immigrants, and to assist those who needed help in reaching their final destinations. Most of the immigrants would be heading for Upper Canada, some for the United States.

Grosse Île and its harbour "form one of the prettiest spots in the river," the Quebec *Gazette* wrote. The harbour, three miles in length and four hundred to six hundred yards wide, bounded by Grosse and three other small islands, was said to be capable of accommodating more than 100 vessels. Troops arrived at Grosse Île in April to set up the quarantine station, and temporarily occupied the only farmhouse on the island, "to the terror of the farmer and his family." A hospital and sheds were hastily built to accommodate immigrants. The inspection station was staffed with three doctors, a marine boarding officer, nurses, clerks, labourers, and troops.

Every ship sailing up the Saint Lawrence from across the Atlantic was to stop at Grosse Île. If no sickness was found among the crew and passengers, and if it was declared that there had been none during the voyage, a ship could then proceed to Quebec. If there were sickness, a ship was to be quarantined for anywhere from three to 30 days, depending on the nature of the illness. Immigrants from the hold and steerage of the quarantined ships were to be put ashore to wash themselves and their luggage, and be fumigated. The ship was also to be fumigated. Cabin passengers, if there was no illness among them, were allowed to remain on board. It was felt that they did

not present a risk because they had not been exposed to the damp, dark, airless filth, stench, sickness and astoundingly overcrowded conditions of those below deck.

At Quebec, and more belatedly at Montreal, the health boards set up further defences. At Quebec, health wardens were appointed for each of the town's 14 wards, with power to enforce the board's regulations. Every house was to be inspected three times a week. Householders were required to "scrape, wash and cleanse their premises and carry away all the filth" that had accumulated during the winter. Buildings were to be purified with lime and whitewash.

Overwhelmed by ships bringing hundreds, and sometimes thousands of immigrants almost every day, the defences broke down. Some ships landed at Quebec without stopping at Grosse Île. Sickness went unreported, undetected, sometimes deliberately hidden. It did not matter in any event, because the procedures were powerless to stop the arrival and spread of cholera. They were futile because no one knew how the cholera was carried and spread.

Medical authorities strongly disagreed about whether cholera was contagious. There seemed more agreement that it was spread in the fetid, warm summer air, the miasma, as it was called. That seemed logical, since the summer air in the towns of Canada was typically ripe with the mixed scent from outdoor privies, garbage, and manure. At Montreal, a notice posted by the Board of Health described "Low and marshy ground, stagnant waters filled with all the elements of miasma," and even in the centre of town "all manner of impurity, animal and vegetable substances in a state of putrescence, and acted on by all the fiercest power of a burning sun."

Conditions at York and its ice-covered harbour were described by the *Canadian Freeman* on April 15: "All the filth of the town—dead horses, dogs, cats, Manure &c. [are] heaped up together on the ice, to drop down, in a few days into the water which is used by almost all the inhabitants of the bay shore." When the ice had melted, the *Freeman* reported on May 17 that "Stagnant pools of water, green as a leek, and emitting deadly exhalations are to be met with in every corner of the town—yards and cellars send forth a stench from rotten vegetables sufficient almost of itself to produce a plague, and the state of the bay, from which a large proportion of inhabitants are supplied with water, is horrible."

No one knew that it was not in this foul air that the disease was spread, but in drinking water. No one then knew that the cholera bug, a bacterium called *Vibro cholerae,* resided in the stool of those infected and, like such bugs, prospered in the warmth of summer. The stool, and sometimes the vomit, of the carriers infected drinking water. It is only by drinking infected water or, more rarely at the time, by eating infected food that people are stricken with cholera. That is the only way this bug enters the human body. With outhouses crowded in the towns of the early

In Toronto, "All the filth of the town—dead horses, dogs, cats, manure are heaped on the ice to drop down into water used by almost all the inhabitants of the bay shore."

nineteenth century, and drinking water drawn from shallow wells that were easily contaminated, it seems hardly surprising that the water became infected. And perhaps even less surprising that drinking water on the notorious coffin ships was also contaminated, causing sickness and often death even before the ships reached shore.

Another important thing the medical authorities did not know is that there were seemingly healthy carriers, people whose feces carried *Vibro cholerae,* but who showed no cholera symptoms. Thus checking for sick people at Grosse Île provided no defence.

The bug lands

The quarantine facilities at Grosse Island were still being set up when the first immigrant ship of 1832 arrived on April 28. She was the *Constantia,* and brought 141 Irish from Limerick, having lost 29 who died of cholera on the voyage. Six weeks later, 400 ships brought 20,000 immigrants, some of them illegally bypassing Grosse Île to land their passengers at Quebec, according to historian Geoffrey Bilson in *A Darkened House: Cholera in Nineteenth-Century Canada.* In just four days, June 2 to 5, a total of 7,151 passed through Grosse Île. Not all had been inspected before proceeding to Quebec. By late Fall, a record 52,000 arrived at Quebec, most from Ireland.

No one really knows which ship first

brought cholera to North America, or exactly when. Many histories give that credit to the brig *Carricks,* which arrived at Grosse Île from Dublin on Sunday, June 3, with 104 immigrants, after having lost 42 passengers to cholera on the voyage. But was it *Carricks?*

On May 8—24 days before *Carricks* reached Grosse Île—the *Quebec* Gazette stated: "An idle report was circulated this morning that some cases of cholera had appeared in the vessels recently arrived at Grosse Île. The rumour, we are happy to say, is groundless." Or was it? A similar rumour was later also denied, only to be proven correct.

On Wednesday, June 6, three days after *Carricks* arrived at Grosse Île, Quebec "was thrown into a great alarm this morning by a report of two persons having died at Grosse Île of cholera," the Montreal *Vindicator* reported. Quebec Health Commissioner Dr. Joseph Morrin, and Health Board Secretary T.A. Young, went to Grosse Île that day to investigate. Morin concluded that "the fever" at Grosse Île was "in no particular different from many now in the Emigrant Hospital" in Quebec, and that in neither case was the fever cholera. The rumour of three cholera patients at Grosse Île "is entirely without foundation," declared the *Gazette* the next day, while the rumoured cholera death at Quebec "is also entirely without foundation." But the rumours were right.

The next day, Thursday, June 7, *Europe,* landed 371 Irish immigrants at Quebec, some of them said to be "labouring under the small pox." *Europe* had not stopped at Grosse Île. A Quebec medical officer, on assurance from the ship's captain that there was no cholera aboard, had issued a licence for *Europe* to enter the harbour and discharge her passengers. "We have heard it stated," said the Quebec *Gazette,* "that a committee of the board of health has been appointed to report on the conduct of the Health Officer in that respect."

On Friday, the steamboat *Voyageur,* landed at Quebec some of the passengers that *Carricks* had brought to Grosse Île four days earlier. The rest of the *Carricks* immigrants continued on the *Voyageur* to Montreal. Two patients died at the Immigrant Hospital in Quebec that Friday. It would soon be confirmed that they had died of cholera. They were the first acknowledged—if not the first actual—cholera deaths in North America. Had they come to North America aboard the *Carricks?* Or aboard the *Europe?* Or were they among the "many" fever patients whom Morrin had said were at the Immigrant Hospital before either *Carricks* or *Europe* reached Quebec?

On Sunday, three days after Morrin and Young visited Grosse Île and denied the existence of cholera, Dr. John Skey, chief military medical officer for Lower Canada, and other doctors, visited the sick at the Immigrant Hospital. "The truth flashed through our minds," Dr. Skey stated, that these were indeed cholera sufferers. The number of reported cholera deaths at Quebec jumped from two on Friday to 12 on Monday, and 161 within a week.

The bug bites

"No building for the sick is yet provided in the lower town," the *Gazette* noted in reporting Skey's confirmation of cholera at Quebec. "Enormous rents have been asked." The *Gazette* offered Quebecers a word of advice: "Cleanliness about houses and about the person, temperance in drinking, the moderate use of food, no excess of any kind, warm clothing, *and perhaps above all a manful determination to meet the worst, and indeed, a kind of heedlessness about the disease.*"

Voyageur—"a pestilent steamer," according to Montreal Health Commissioner Dr. Robert Nelson—continued her trip from Quebec, bringing the cholera to Montreal, on Sunday, the same day that it had finally been confirmed at Quebec. At Montreal, a sick immigrant from the *Voyageur* "was carried to a tavern on the wharf, where he died," Dr. Nelson, recalled in his 1866 book, *Asiatic Cholera.* "All that night and all the succeeding day, the body of this man was exposed to the gaze of the public, and, actuated by motives of curiosity, many people visited it." The Montreal *Gazette* reported 23 deaths in three days, citing whisky and fear as causes. "The greater proportion of those who died, have been irregular in the habits, or have been guilty of some imprudence." As for milder cases, they were "attributed to the effects of fear operating to produce sickness among the timid." Within two weeks, there were 56 deaths at just one boarding house, and hundreds of others throughout the city.

One day after its appearance at Montreal, the cholera reached Upper Canada, striking at Prescott where there were 16 deaths in two weeks. "Our village is in a dreadful state of consternation," a Prescott correspondent wrote in the *Brockville Recorder* June 17. "Many are removing their families to a distance. The crews of the Government boats between here and Montreal… have deserted. Our Magistrates have purchased all the spare boards in this place, sent a bateau to Drummond's Island, and a number of carpenters to erect sheds for the sick emigrants destined for the upper parts of the province." It hit nearby towns almost immediately, and even country inns and taverns. Seven miles south of Brockville, reported the *Recorder,* "an intemperate man died in one of Mr. McKenzie's out houses."

By June 18, the cholera had reached York, and, with very few exceptions, was in every town and hamlet in Lower and Upper Canada, from Quebec to Niagara. Immigrants crossing from Lower Canada into Vermont brought the disease into the United States, where it spread as far south as the Gulf of Mexico.

The disease struck with explosive energy, especially in Lower Canada. At Quebec, 440 deaths were reported within three weeks; at Montreal, the death rate was greater.

There was initially no accommodation at either Quebec or Montreal for thousands of sick and indigent immigrants. Few had money for hotels or boarding houses, and were unfit to travel to their planned destinations, mostly in Upper Canada. Cholera patients were not admitted to the existing hospitals and "emigrant" hospitals had to be hastily set up. At Montreal, sick immigrants were put in whatever sheds could be found, one offering little better than a roof with a dirt floor, covered with straw on which lay the sick, the dying and the dead.

The dead were buried as fast as possible. There was no time for prayers, mourning, or tombstones. There was fear that some were buried before they were actually dead. At the Catholic burying ground at the St. Antoine suburb, a trench "10 feet wide, 8 feet deep and over 100 feet long" was dug for as many as two hundred bodies, Nelson wrote. "The dead were closely packed there in tiers, three to four deep, and covered over with earth, leaving the remainder of a trench to receive newcomers."

The cholera could have been stopped with clean, safe drinking water. But not knowing that, the great effort was made to clean the air. Hundreds of volunteers in both towns joined citizen committees to clean up the manure and filth that fouled the air. "On Saturday, the Artillery went through the different streets of the town, with several pieces of cannon, and discharged blank cartridge, with the view, if possible, of disinfecting the atmosphere," the Montreal *Gazette* reported on June 19. "In the evening, fires of rosins and other bituminous matter were to be seen in every part of the town." At York, every household was ordered to burn, every day, "pitch, Tar, rosin, Sulphur and any other anti-contagious combustibles." A barrel of tar was provided at "the Court House Yard for the use of such as are too indigent to purchase it for themselves."

At first it was thought, or hoped, that the disease might be confined to the "lower orders," the impoverished immigrants from Ireland, not so much because they were in ill health, ill-fed, ill-clothed and ill-housed, but because, it was felt, of riotous drinking and "irregular habits." The disease knew no boundaries of race, social order or morality, striking the reputable and disreputable alike.

Doctors, clergy and others who attended the sick were particularly hard hit. There were too few doctors; in Montreal, only 15 for a population of 32,000. They were "almost completely exhausted by fatigue," noted the *Vindicator*. The *Quebec Mercury* reported the first doctor killed by cholera on June 16, Dr. C.N. Perrault, secretary of the town's Board of Health and said to be "one of the most skillful Canadian physicians." Brockville, too, lost its Board of Health secretary, the youthful Dr. Robert Gilmour. The first medical casualty in Montreal was reported by the *Gazette* June 19, "Mr. John Grant Struthers, student of medicine." Also noted at Montreal were the deaths of a member of the Legislative Council, a road contractor, a chair maker, and a tavern keeper. In Quebec, the reported toll included a member of the House of Assembly, a judge, a lawyer, and a clock maker.

Dr. Daniel Tracey, physician, very recently elected member of the House of Assembly, and editor and publisher of the *Vindicator,* apologized for publishing only a "half-sheet… on account of the prevailing malady having attacked several of our hands." Tracey wrote that he, too, had "but just recovered from an attack, which we were enabled, by early attention, to arrest." That was published on June 19. Tracey had died June 18.

There was no precise count of the number of 1832 cholera deaths in Canada. The Quebec Board of Health recorded 3,451 in that town, and almost certainly missed some. Dr. Nelson estimated 4,000 at Montreal. Bishop John Strachan estimated 400 at York. There were lesser totals at each of dozens of smaller towns and hamlets. In the Atlantic Provinces, Nova Scotia, Prince Edward Island and Newfoundland all escaped the disease, while only at Saint John, New Brunswick was it reported, with 32 deaths. A widely used estimate of 9,000 Canadian cholera deaths in 1832 seems reasonable.

There was a second, smaller cholera epidemic in 1834, and several more during a period of nearly four decades, with an estimated 20,000 deaths by 1871. But the 1832 pandemic, the first in Canada and North America, was the largest. Yet, 15 years later, far worse was to come when many more Irish immigrants, fleeing the great potato famine, would bring typhus with them.

Readings •Geoffrey Bilson. *A Darkened House: Cholera in Nineteenth-Century Canada.* Toronto: University of Toronto Press, 1980. •C.M. Godfrey. *The Cholera Epidemics in Upper Canada 1832 – 1966.* Toronto: Secombe House, 1968. •Marian A. Patterson. *The Cholera Epidemic of 1832 in York, Upper Canada.* Bulletin of the Medical Library Association: Chicago, April, 1959. •John B. Osborne. *Preparing for the pandemic: city boards of health and the arrival of cholera in Montreal, New York, and Philadelphia in 1832.* Urban History Review: Toronto, 36.2 (Spring 2008). •Robert Nelson. *Asiatic Cholera: the origin and spread in Asia, Africa and Europe, introduction into America through Canada.* New York: William A. Townsend, 1866. •W. Marsden. *An essay on the Contagion, Infection, Portability and Communicability of Asiatic Cholera in its relations to Quarantine; with a brief History of its Origin and Course in Canada, from 1832.* Canada Medical Journal: Montreal, vol. IV no. 11 (May 1868).

Newspapers (1837). Brockville *Recorder.* Montreal: *Canadian Courant, Gazette, Vindicator.* Niagara *Gleaner.* Quebec *Gazette.* Toronto *Canadian Freeman.*

20,000 Irish die fleeing to Canada in 1847 famine

Ireland lost a quarter of her population to the great famine, from 1845 to 1850. There are no accurate figures, but as many as 1.5 million perished, including many of more than one million who emigrated to England, Scotland, North America and elsewhere in the famine years. Only the United States took more Irish refugees than Canada, and the United States took care to accept the healthiest and least distressed. One hundred thousand Irish sailed for Canada in 1847; as many as 20,000 perished, mostly from typhus. Canadian doctors, nurses, clergy and others sacrificed their lives in heroic efforts to save or help the refugees.

The plight of the Irish

Ireland, in the census year of 1841, was a country of at least 8.2 million people, "On the verge of starving, her population rapidly increasing, three-quarters of her labourers unemployed, housing conditions appalling, and the standard of living unbelievably low," historian Cecil Woodham Smith writes in *The Great Hunger.* Two-thirds of the Irish, most of them tenants of the great landowners, lived on potatoes grown on small plots of land. Potatoes were fed to people, pigs and cows, providing, at best, a diet of potatoes, milk and meat. "In many districts, their only food is the potato, their only beverage water," William Courtenay, Earl of Devon, wrote in an 1845 Royal Commission report. "Their cabins are seldom a protection against the weather… a bed and a blanket is a rare luxury… and nearly in all their pig and a manure heap constitute their only property."

Hunger was common, especially in the summer months when there were no old potatoes left and new ones not ready for picking. Then there were the famine years: 23 potato crop failures during a span of 118 years. None were as bad as the famine that struck with a potato blight on September 1845, and peaked in 1847. Before the blight hit, the fields were green with the promise of a bumper crop of potatoes. With great suddenness, "The leaves were all scorched black," a relief official wrote. "It was the work of a night."

British Prime Minister Robert Peel

Mount Stewart House, County Down, Northern Ireland, home of Charles William Vane, Lord Londonderry, now a tourist attraction. Vane spent £150,000 renovating it. He contributed just £30 to the local relieve committee while his tenants starved during the Great Hunger. The Connemara cabin on Ireland's west coast, shown below, is typical of many of the one-room, dirt floor Irish tenant cabins during the great Irish famine of 1845-50.

averted tragedy in the first famine year. He paid £100,000 to buy corn from the United States and launched public works that employed half a million people. "No man died of famine during his administration," acknowledged the Irish *Freeman's Journal.* It was during the 1846-1852 administration of Prime Minister John Russell that 2.5 million Irish perished or emigrated.

To feed themselves, the Irish sold or pawned whatever they could. "A stranger would wonder how these wretched beings find food," a policeman wrote. "Clothes being in pawn, there is nothing to change. They sleep in their rags and have pawned their bedding." But still they perished. "The people died by the roadside with grass in their mouths," wrote Canadian Catholic historian John Gallagher.

Yet "Huge quantities of food were exported from Ireland to England throughout

London Illustrated News, August 12, 1843. Image courtesy Steve Taylor, "Views of the Famine," http://adminstaff.vassar.edu/sttaylor/FAMINE/

the period when the people of Ireland were starving," Woodham Smith wrote. People starved because they had no money. "The face of the country is covered with ripe corn while the people dread starvation," wrote an official in Limerick. "The grain will go out of the country, sold to pay rent."

The Russell government saw the answer to an over-populated and underfed Ireland in emigration, larger and more productive farms, and the unrestrained operation of free market capitalism. The policies were applied with criminal disregard of human life; fueled by racial and religious animosity; exacerbated by the ruthlessness of too many landlords, and an economic depression in England. Charles Trevelyan, the government official in charge of relief, despised the Irish. "The great evil with which we have to contend is not the physical evil of the famine," he wrote, "but the moral evil of the selfish, perverse and turbulent character of the people." He also claimed that "The judgment of God sent the calamity to teach the Irish a lesson."

The Russell government cancelled the Peel program of public works and distribution of food. In their place it relied on workhouses and soup kitchens. Workhouses housed entire families in conditions not much better than jail, but could not begin to accommodate the bursting number of the destitute and hungry. The government soup kitchens lasted barely more than 18 months, shut down in the summer of 1847. The Irish were intended to live on the fall crop of potatoes. That fall crop was the smallest of the famine years, less than one-seventh the size of the 1844 crop, before the blight hit. The worst of the starvation started.

At the same time, the *Poor Law Amendment Act* placed the entire burden of relief on the shoulders of the landlords, who were now to collect not only their rents, but £10 million in taxes. It was utterly impossible. Money could not be collected from millions of people who had none. Some landlords were still very wealthy, but with little or no rent, many were on the brink of bankruptcy.

To help landlords collect blood from stone, the government provided troops, and instructions. "Arrest, remand, do anything you can" to collect taxes, Charles Wood, chancellor of the Exchequer told George Villiers (Lord Clarendon), the top British official in Ireland. "Send horse, foot and dragoons," Wood added. "I should not be at all squeamish as to what I did, to the verge of the law and a little beyond." The tax collectors seized livestock, furniture, tools, even clothing, managing to collect property worth less than £1 million.

Government policies gave landlords every incentive to ship their destitute tenants far away. One of the first to do so was Denis Mahon, a major in the British cavalry who had inherited 9,000 acres and 28 tiny villages in County Roscommon. Mahon spent £4,000 to send 800 of his tenants to Canada. They were promised agents would meet them in Canada and provide money, clothing and assistance. Other landlords made the same promises. Almost all were lies.

When others tenants refused to leave, Mahon evicted 3,000. They were among the first of half a million torn from their homes, children screaming, mothers weeping, one woman still clinging to her torn-away doorpost. Cottages and cabins were torn down; pottery, beds and clothing confiscated. The homeless were left to survive in "scalps," holes dug two or three feet deep and roofed with twigs and turf, or bigger holes covered with the timber from tumbled homes. Troops hated evicting. A detachment of highlanders gave money to people they evicted.

Lord (Henry) Brougham, an acerbic Scot and former Lord Chancellor of Great Britain, defended the right of landlords to treat their tenants like cattle. "Property would be valueless and capital would no longer be invested in the cultivation of the land" if landlords could not do as they wished with their land and their tenants, he told the House of Lords in London.

Charity

Private charity, in Ireland and from around the world, tried to rectify the criminal conditions created by the public sector. In Ireland, everyone from school children to landlords either donated or helped raise funds—although one absentee landlord limited his kitchen soup donation to £1. A Church of Ireland minister gave a daily pint of soup to 1,149 people; a Belfast committee gave daily soup to more than 12,000. Queen Victoria, the Pope and the U.S. President made personal donations. Victoria issued two fund-raising appeals to the English, who responded with £200,000. Irish soldiers in Calcutta sent £14,000. Ottoman Sultan Abdülmecid sent £1,000 and three shiploads of food. The Choctaw Indi-

Bridget O'Donnel and her children, Irish famine victims. *Illustrated London News,* December 22, 1849.

ans of Oklahoma, who had faced starvation 16 years earlier, sent $710. The rector of the Irish College in Rome sold his horse and gig to make his donation. Catholic priests and parishioners alike sent large amounts of money.

The most effective relief organization was a special committee of the Friends of Society, the Quakers. Quaker aid amounted to £200,000, but more important were the Quaker volunteers who operated soup kitchens where they were most needed. At least 15 of the Quaker volunteers died of typhus. The Quakers neither preached nor proselytized, but Catholic priests condemned parishioners who accepted Protestant food.

Heroic though it was, private aid provided only buckets of help in an ocean of need. "The condition of our country has not improved in spite of the great exertions made by charitable bodies," the Quaker committee wrote to Prime Minister Russell. The need, it said, was "...far beyond the reach of private exertion, the Government alone could raise the funds and carry the measures necessary in many districts to save the lives of the people."

"The people sink," wrote an Irish official; "they have no stamina left, they say, 'It is the Will of God,' and they die."

Coffin ships

All the coffin ships were sailing vessels. Paddle wheel steamships plied rivers and coastal waters, and steamships were now starting to cross the Atlantic. Fourteen years earlier, the Canadian wooden paddle wheeler *Royal William,* was the first under steam alone, carrying Nova Scotia coal and seven passengers on a 25-day voyage to Gravesand on the Thames River, England. In 1840, Nova Scotia's Sam Cunard, an investor in the *Royal William,* launched the British and North American Steam Packet Company, the ancestor of the Cunard line that dominated trans-Atlantic passenger service for a century, including the famous *Queen Mary* and *Queen Elizabeth* ships.

The coffin ships carried timber to Britain in their holds, and on the westward backhaul, in place of ballast, they carried as many as 600 refugees in their holds, the ship owners happy to get extra revenue from very low fares. A few passengers sometimes travelled in the relative comfort and safety of deck cabins. Those in the holds died from typhus, dysentery, diarrhea, and malnutrition, but mostly typhus.

Typhus is carried by lice, which flourish in unsanitary conditions. More unsanitary conditions could hardly be found than in the grim holds of the coffin ships. Typhus was fatal to as many as half who caught the fever in the 1847 exodus to Canada.

The 300-ton barque *Elizabeth and Sarah* was typical. The 85-year-old tub carried 64 more passengers and crew than her legal limit of 212 on her voyage from Killala, Ireland, to Quebec. She had 32 bunks for 276 passengers. She was required by regulations to carry 12,532 gallons of water, but carried only, 8,700. The required weekly ration of seven pounds of bread, biscuits, flour or oatmeal for each steerage passenger was also short, as it was on many coffin ships. Below decks there were no sanitary facilities, little light or ventilation. Forty emigrants died on the voyage. The *Elizabeth and Sarah* broke down as it entered the broad St. Lawrence. Alexander Buchanan, Canada's chief emigration officer, had her towed to the Grosse Île quarantine station near Quebec, at his own expense.

A prominent Quebec resident and businessman, Buchanan was dedicated in his efforts to help emigrants with information about transportation, employment, land purchase, and protection against unscrupulous employers, merchants, and fraudsters. On occasion he paid the steamship fare to Montreal, Kingston or Toronto for emigrants intending to settle in Canada, rather than moving to the United States, and provided additional food, until overwhelmed by the need.

If coffin-ship typhus wasn't bad enough, hundreds more perished in shipwrecks. One ship, sailing from Ireland, sank before it was out of sight of those on land. The *Exmouth,* bound from Londonderry to Quebec with 240 immigrants and 11 crew, sank after striking the Isle of Islay in the Scottish Hebrides during a gale, the Quebec *Morning Chronicle* reported May 17. All perished except three seamen who made it to a cleft in the rocky coast. The Toronto *Globe* reported the wreck of the *Crofton* off the west coast of Scotland, "…with the loss of 400 emigrants."

The *Globe,* with a tinge of tragic comedy, reported the story of the *Swatara.* She "was driven on the coast of the Isle of Man in a gale, and to save the ship the masts were cut away. Having refitted, she sailed for the United States. In a few days, off the south of Ireland, she again lost one of her masts, and, with several of the emigrants on board dead, put into an Irish port. Having again refitted, she recently sailed a second time for her destination. Intelligence has been received that the unfortunate ship has put into Derry, having lost her masts a third time, and with more of the passengers dead."

Emigration

The Irish who emigrated[1] to North America during the four famine years 1846-49 emigrated mostly to the United States. They may have been starving, but they'd had a bellyful of British rule, and wanted no more of it.

Official British figures for those four years say that 632,076 people (mostly Irish) left the British Isles for the United States, and 225,552 for British North America, i.e., the Maritime colonies and Canada. Emigration to British North America peaked at 109,680 in 1847, while 142,154 sailed to the United States. Probably 100,000 of those who emigrated to British North America that year were Irish. And of these, an estimated 15,000 sailed for Saint John, New Brunswick, and 85,000 for Grosse Île and

[1]The terms "emigration" and "emigrant" are used here rather than "immigration" and "immigrant," for the sake of consistency. All contemporary accounts refer exclusively to emigrants; their hospitals and sheds were also all emigrant hospitals and emigrant sheds.

A 46-foot granite Celtic cross, the Irish Memorial National Historic Site, at Grosse Île, commemorates the Irish famine refugees who died in Canada. An inscription reads: "Thousands of the children of the Gael were lost on this island while fleeing foreign tyrannical laws and artificial famine in the years 1847-8. God bless them. God bless Ireland. Erected by the Ancient Order of the Hibernians in America, 1909."

Quebec's entry port to Canada.

But whether from New Brunswick or from Canada, many sought to flee to the United States as fast as they could. They were far from welcomed.

If the Irish, especially the Catholic Irish, were detested by many in England, they were hardly less so in the United States. Antipathy rose from a perceived burden and risk imposed by destitute people; from sectarian conflict; from ethnic bigotry; and from fear that cheap foreign labour posed a threat to American workers. In Philadelphia, the City of Brotherly Love, a church, a seminary and houses were burned in three days of anti-Irish rioting in 1844. Thirteen people were killed, and a greater number wounded.

At the crest of the tide of famine refugees, the United States sought to prevent the most destitute both from sailing to U.S. ports, and from crossing from British North America to American soil. When an 1847 law reduced by one-third the number of passengers permitted on ships sailing for U.S. ports, the Quebec *Chronicle*, May 5, 1847 presciently saw it as an effort "to check the influx of emigrants to the states. The immediate effect will be to raise fares and divert a larger portion of the multitude from the Union to British America."

And that's what happened. American ships were more comfortable, healthier and safer than the British coffin ships, but the fare was more than three times as great. U.S. state and port authorities also took measures aimed at preventing the aged, sick and destitute from disembarking on U.S. soil. "To the United States go the people of good character and in comfortable circumstances; to British North America, the evil and ill-disposed," wrote the U.S. consul in Londonderry. "They go to Canada either because the fare is cheaper or their landlords are getting rid of them."

Equally stern were the efforts to prevent the famine refugees in Canada and New Brunswick from crossing the border. They were refused aboard ships heading to U.S. ports from Saint John, and from Canada through Lake Champlain. Officials at U.S. border customs turned the Irish back. At Lewiston, New York, an official who allowed Irish ferry passengers to disembark on American soil was jailed.

It was all to no avail. There were hundreds of miles of border where even the destitute and sick could enter the United States undetected, and many thousands did. Some men left their wives and children in Canada, promising to send for them once there were established in the United States. Some wives never heard from them.

CANADA 1847

Grosse Île

From the start of 1847 there was widespread apprehension in both Quebec and Montreal that the year would bring a deluge of famine refugees, with a risk of typhus, the fever, as it was generally called. In March, a Quebec citizens' committee sent a petition to colonial secretary Earl Grey in London, seeking help to prepare for the deluge. The Montreal *Gazette* warned that Canada was about to be "inundated with an enormous crowd of poor and destitute emigrants." Yet the government did almost nothing to prepare the ill-equipped Grosse Île quarantine station.

Dr. George Mellis Douglas knew about crises at Grosse Île. During the 1832 cholera panic he was assistant to the station's medical director, and four years later he was the medical director. On February 19, Douglas asked Governor General Lord Elgin (James Bruce) for £3,000 to prepare the station for a record number of emigrants. He was given £300, the use of a small steamer, the *St. George,* to ply between Grosse Île and Quebec, and authority to hire a sailing vessel for not more than £25.

The first emigrant ship of the year, the *Syria* from Liverpool, dropped anchor at

Grosse Île at 4:30 p.m. on May 14. She arrived with 241 passengers, all Irish, nine having died on the voyage. Douglas found 84 typhus patients aboard the *Syria,* and expected another 20 to 24 to come down with the fever.

The number of patients from the first ship approached the station hospital's intended capacity of 150. Ten thousand more were already on their way. Three days before the *Syria* arrived, Buchanan issued a list of vessels that had left for Quebec between April 3 and 17. "It appears there are now on their way to this port, 34 vessels, having on board 10,636 passengers," the *Morning Chronicle* summarized. All but one of the ships, the *Favourite* from Glasgow, came from Irish ports or from Liverpool, a major port of embarkation for the Irish. Almost all would be Irish. The number of passengers on each ship varied from 80 aboard the *Favourite* to 580 aboard the *John Bolton* from Liverpool.

If 241 emigrants and a little more than 100 fever patients represented about half the Grosse Île hospital capacity, how could it handle ten thousand? It couldn't. Yet more than twice that number would crowd the island.

By the end of May there were 40 vessels lined up at Grosse Île, with some 13,000 passengers. In a letter dated June 2 published in the Quebec *Mercury,* Dr. Douglas says there were 1,100 patients housed in "hospitals, schools, churches and tents," with "six medical men in attendance." There had been 116 deaths, while "The number of orphans does not exceed twenty." The orphans, he said, were "…specially cared for, and receive milk and nourish-

ment… There is no distress from want of food," with the daily ration of one pound per person. In addition, the ever helpful Alexander Buchanan sent a steamer with additional biscuits, oatmeal, soft bread, tea, sugar and pork for "the most unfortunate."

Matters, however, were rapidly worsening. Grosse Île became crowded with as many as 25,000 emigrants. The line of waiting ships grew longer. The ships were quarantined for as long as 12 weeks. The longer the refugees were held on the waiting ships, the more the fever spread. Despite a prohibition, many bodies were said to have been dumped overboard, while other bodies from the ships were among the 5,424 buried on Grosse Île.

It was impossible to hold 25,000 people for an effective four-week quarantine period. Many were released early; 4,000 to 5,000 on one particular Sunday in June; 2,000 of whom Dr. Douglas expected to fall ill within three weeks. "Good God!" he wrote in a letter, warning authorities. "What evils will befall the city wherever they alight?"

The last of 398 emigrant ships to stop at Grosse Île in 1847 was the *Richard Watson* on November 7. Forty-three ships are thought to have unloaded their passengers at Quebec without stopping at Grosse Île. The quarantine station was able to offer but little help to the sick immigrants, and no effective quarantine protection to Canada.

Up the river

From Grosse Île, up the river and across Lake Ontario, came tens of thousands of the unfortunate Irish, thousands of them to die at Quebec, Montreal, Kingston, Toronto,

Niagara, and elsewhere.

In Quebec, the *Morning Chronicle* warned that "Something must be done by ourselves, and that immediately, or else the whole city will be one general hospital," July 27.

While the great majority of the Irish who left Grosse Île sailed directly for Montreal, Quebec had its ample share of sickness, death, and stench. In addition to the refugees who did land at Quebec, there was constant travel between the city and the quarantine station during the entire quarantine period. It started the day after the first quarantine ship, the *Syria,* arrived, when the ship's captain and a passenger visited Quebec.

What was needed at Quebec was a hospital for its own patients. The city's Marine and Emigrant Hospital, by late July, was crammed full of Irish refugees, Quebec patients had been turned away, and the city had no other hospital. "The disease is spreading in the suburbs and coves, and will soon reach the heart of the city," said the *Chronicle.*

At a citizens' meeting the day before, the mayor, doctors, clergy, and merchants clamoured for use of the city's parliament building for a hospital. The building had housed the legislature of Lower Canada until 1841 when Lower and Upper Canada were combined under one government. The capital of what was now officially called Canada East and Canada West was, in 1847, located in Montreal. (Two year's later, Montreal's parliament building was burned down in two days of rioting and the peripatetic capital moved again, eventually to Ottawa).

The day after the *Chronicle* sounded its plea for a hospital for Quebec citizens, word from Montreal was reached that Governor General Bruce had approved the use of one of the buildings of the Cavalry Barracks, lying outside of the barrack gates on the Plains of Abraham, for a city hospital. "The citizens will be provided with a temporary receptacle for their sick poor, in an excellent location," said the *Chronicle.*

Still the crisis grew. By August 16, no more burials were to be allowed at the burying ground near the Emigrant and Marine hospital since the grounds were "full of bodies, emitting a most noisome effluvia, highly dangerous to the health of the citizens." During the week, three children—two aged five and one 2-1/2 years—died on the city's wharves. One man from Grosse Île arrived with his dead wife, wrapped in a blanket.

On July 21, a soup kitchen was busy feeding some 200 emigrant families, but two kitchen employees "have fallen sick from the fever."

The *Chronicle* appealed for help for the growing number of orphans at Grosse Île: "We are confident that these helpless little wanderers… will be cared for and protected by those of our citizens who have been blessed with enough to spare of this world's goods."

Montreal

Some 80,000 Irish landed at Montreal, most of them later moving farther up the river and across lake Ontario. They were doctored by Montreal doctors, nursed by the Order of Grey Nuns, attended by Catholic and Protestant clergy. Housed at first in emigrant sheds in the heart of the city, left-

F.H. Granger, 1849. *Robertson's Landmarks of Toronto,* Vol. 3, p. 346. Toronto: J. Ross Robertson, 1898

Toronto harbour, where 38,560 Irish famine emigrants landed on a city of 20,000 in 1847.

over from the 1832 cholera epidemic, they were moved in August to a new hospital and more extensive sheds at Point St. Charles, a short distance upstream.

When an Irish woman gave birth to a baby in Montreal, the Grey Nuns placed it in a hospital room with 18 other orphans. The mother may have perished, or very possibly, struggling to keep herself alive, was unable to support her infant. It was "apparently healthy," the Montreal *Pilot* reported. Yet it came down with the fever, affected others, and 10 of the 19 orphans died.

Typhus claimed 3,579 victims in Montreal according to the official count of the Executive Council. In the chaotic situation, the official count likely missed a good many deaths. An inscription on Montreal's "Black Rock" claims a much higher total.

Irish workers building the Victoria Bridge across the St. Lawrence 12 years later, were unnerved by the discovery of a mass grave in Windmill Point, near where the Point St. Charles emigration hospital and sheds had stood. On December 1, 1859, they inscribed on the boulder: "To Preserve from Desecration the Remains of 6000 Immigrants Who died of Ship Fever A.D. 1847-48 This Stone is erected by the Workmen of Messrs. Peto, Brassey and Betts Employed in the Construction of the Victoria Bridge A.D. 1859."

Toronto

A city of some 20,000 bordered by forest and Lake Ontario, Toronto received, from May to November, 38,560 Irish emigrants at Reese's Wharf, as noted by historians

Mark McGowan and Michael Chard. Most passed through Toronto for scattered settlements, as near as Hamilton or as far as London or Niagara, where many fled to the United States (including the grandfather of car maker Henry Ford). Of fewer than 3,000 that remained in the city by year's end, more than 1,100 lay buried in three graveyards.

Toronto set up a Board of Health to care for the emigrants and protect Torontonians from their diseases. Cabs and carters were told not to move into the city any who appeared ill; local residents, hotels and even the General Hospital were prohibited from accommodating them. A new hospital was prepared for Torontonians and the General Hospital became the Emigrant Hospital.

Jane Black, from Limerick, was the year's first emigrant ship to dock at Toronto, on May 23. The tide of emigrants quickly swelled. On June 8, the *City of Toronto* brought 700 to its namesake city. One thousand were reported to have arrived aboard the *Sovereign* on July 6. The facilities at Reese's Wharf were soon overwhelmed, and the new emigrant hospital had to be enlarged. By August, almost 700 patients crowded the Emigrant Hospital and many more sat in 14 sheds hastily built (by a contractor for $250 each) on the hospital grounds. The sheds were opened-sided roofs, some 50 by 10 feet, most 75 by 20 feet. With rows of benches, they were shelters from summer heat and rain for emigrants who waited for admittance to the hospital, to the burying grounds, or to be hustled out of Toronto.

Among emigrant stories, none are more poignant than that of the Willis family, related by McGowan and Chard. Parents and five children boarded the *Jessie* at Limerick, Ireland on April 18. Before the ship weighed anchor, one son fell ill, and was left behind for an early death. An 18-year-old-son and a 10-year-old daughter died on the 56-day Atlantic crossing. Another daughter died at Grosse Île. At Brantford, their final destination, 90 kilometres southwest of Toronto, typhus claimed the father and the remaining son. Only the mother survived.

In the 1848 census, the Irish were 39 percent of Toronto's 23,505 people, the largest ethnic group, more than the English and Scots combined, according to Catholic historian D.S. Shea. By now, some of the Irish who had passed through in 1847 had returned to establish their homes in Toronto. Not all Toronto welcomed them. Among those who did not was George Brown, the Scottish journalist and politician, a leading crusader for "responsible government," founder and editor of the powerful *Globe* newspaper, and an undoubted bigot. "Irish beggars are to be met everywhere, and they are as ignorant and vicious as they are poor," he wailed in the *Globe.* "They are lazy, improvident, and unthankful; they fill our poorhouses and our prisons, and are as brutish in their superstitions as Hindoos."

Saint John

Of the 15,000 who sailed for Saint John, 800 died aboard their coffin ships, 600 died and were buried on Partridge Isle quarantine station, and 595 died in the city's poorhouse, Catholic historian Rev. John A. Gallagher reported.

When the first ship, the *Eliza Liddell,* arrived in July, it was greeted with storms of protests about the conditions of the refugees, widows, small children, and the elderly, destitute and sick. The *Aeolus* was the last to arrive, in November. She was one of nine ships that carried displaced Irish tenants from the Sligo estate of a future British prime minister, Lord Palmerston (John Temple).

The city council wrote to Palmerston to "deeply regret" that he "…or his authorized agent should have exposed such a numerous and distressed portion of his tenantry to the severity and privations of a New Brunswick winter… unprovided with the common means of support, with broken down constitutions, and almost in a state of nudity." It is doubtful, wrote Woodham Smith, that Palmerston was aware of the conditions in which his tenants were shipped by his agents.

Those who gave their lives

The scores of Canadian doctors, nurses, clergy and other who gave their lives trying to save or help the famine refugees varied from a bishop to at least one immigration officer.

Dr. Benson of Dublin, where he had worked with typhus patients, was probably the first. He arrived as a cabin passenger on aboard the *Wandsworth* on May 21, volunteered to help the doctors on Grosse Île, and died six days later. Among the deaths of other caregivers reported by the *Chronicle*, on July 16 there was "Rev. W. Chaderston, who has worked 12 hours a day "in attendance upon the sea faring men and emigrants" at Quebec's Marine and Emigrant hospital. The next day, in Montreal, it was Dr. McGale, an assistant physician who left "a widow and a large family of children, entirely destitute."

Historian John Gallagher's says 44 Catholic priests and 17 Anglican ministers served on Grosse Île, and seven of them died. At Montreal, three priests and 17 Grey Nuns working in the hospitals perished. "There are at the present moment 48 nuns sick from exposure, fatigue and attacks of the disease," the Montreal *Pilot* reported July 8. The fever claimed the life of Montreal's popular mayor, John Mills, who visited the fever hospital and sheds regularly. A priest and a nun perished at Kingston.

Prominent among those who fell in Toronto were Roman Catholic Bishop Michael Power; Dr. George Grassett, chief medical officer at the Emigrant Hospital; and Edward McElderry, the emigration agent who met all the arriving refugees at Reese's Wharf.

Many seamen caught the fever on the coffin ships and perished—including at least two captains reported by the *Chronicle,* the skippers of the *Sisters* and *Paragon.* Also, "The lady of the doctor of the *Goliath* died."

Was this genocide?

The British treatment of the Irish has been described as genocide, not only by the Irish but also by others, including some American historians. Judged by today's international rules there can be little doubt that Britain would have at least been investigated by the Canadian-initiated International Criminal Court. But if genocide it was, it was no greater than the genocide of American Indians by American settlers, among scores of genocides from the eighteenth to twenty-first centuries.

It was little enough, but the continuing impoverishment of the Irish was somewhat alleviated in the decades following the famine. Ireland's population fell from 8.2 million in the 1841 census to 6.5 million a decade later, some larger farms became more productive, "In some respects, death and clearance improved," Woodham Smith writes after 400 pages chronicling details of the disaster. Even housing conditions improved: "Nearly 300,000 mud huts disappeared."

This could have been accomplished, and much greater achieved by the government's vaunted free market capitalism, without the death of more than a million Irish—were it not for the disregard of human life, the greed of landlords, sectarian persecution, ethnic animosity, and ignorance. Capitalism may be like the fire that heats our homes, drives our cars and flies our planes. Both fuel great benefits, but only when properly controlled.

Readings

André Charbonneau. *Grosse Île and the Irish Memorial National Historical Site of Canada.* Parks Canada. www.pc.gc.ca/eng/lhn-nhs/qc/**grosseile**/natcul/natcul1/a.aspx Accessed May 5, 2012.

John A. Gallagher, Rev. *The Irish Emigration of 1847 and its Canadian Consequences.* Canadian Catholic Historical Association, Report 3 (1936), pp 43-57.

The History Place. *Irish Potato Famine. Financial ruin.* http://www.historyplace.com/worldhistory/famine/ruin.htm. *Irish Potato Famine. Coffin Ships.* http://www.historyplace.com/worldhistory/famine/ruin.htm. Access May 5, 2012.

Mark G. McGown and Michael Chard. *Historical background.* Ireland Park Foundation, Toronto Irish Famine Memorial. http://www.irelandparkfoundation.com/index.php?p=1_1 Accessed May 14, 2012.

Marianopolis College. *Immigration. Quebec history.* http://faculty.marianopolis.edu/c.belanger/quebechistory/encyclopedia/ImmigrationHistoryofCanada.htm

D.S. Shea, Rev. *The Irish Immigrant Adjustment to Toronto: 1840-1860.* Canadian Catholic Historical Society, Study Sessions, 39 (1972), pp 53-60.

Cecil Woodham Smith. *The Great Hunger.* London, New English Library edition, 1977.

University College Cork, Ireland. *Famine & Religion: Ireland under the Union, 1815-1870. Responses to the famine. Private relief work, abroad and at home.* http://multitext.ucc.ie/d/Private_Responses_to_the_Famine33443611812. Accessed May 19, 2012.

Wikipedia. Great Famine (Ireland). http://en.wikipedia.org/wiki/Irish_potato_famine. Accessed May 5, 2012.

Newspapers: *Illustrated London News.* (1847 January 16, Famine and Starvation in the County of Cork. 1848 December 16, Evictions of the Peasantry in Ireland. 1849, December 22, Condition of Ireland. 1850 July 6, official British figures on annual number of emigrants sailing to North America, 1825 to 1849.) Quebec *Morning Chronicle.* Toronto *Globe.* Montreal *Herald.*

CHAPTER TEN
Booze

When children drank whisky at breakfast

For more than a century-and-a-half, Europeans had been killing North America's Indians by giving them firewater—whisky, brandy, rum, port, sherry—in exchange for furs. Now, in the first decades of the nineteenth century, Canada's pioneer settlers were killing themselves with their own medicine.

Alcohol consumption had reached epidemic proportions, and it was taking a terrible toll. At Ancaster, in Upper Canada, 11 of 13 accidental deaths in 1829 were attributed to excessive drinking. Inquests in the Bathurst District blamed all 20 accidental deaths on booze, according to a study on pioneer drinking habits by Rev. M.A. Garland and historian J.J. Talman.

With an abundant number of distilleries—the Bathurst District alone had six in 1836—whisky was plentiful and cheap. Farmers supplied the distilleries with grain. One bushel of grain made three or three-and-a-half gallons of whisky. The farmer received half the whisky as payment for his grain. Whatever he and his family

William B. Edwards. Library and Archives Canada. PA-080920

didn't drink, was sold to inns, taverns and the many shops that served as drinking houses.[1]

Whisky was a solace in the isolated log cabins where settlers lived harsh and lonely lives of incredible toil. "In many families," wrote Garland and Tallman, "whisky was served to each member of the household every morning, and thus from infancy, the children were accustomed to its taste." The whisky was often diluted with water, especially for young children. It was, however, considered a necessary protection against the winter's cold or the summer's heat, and an energizing tonic to help workers—men, women and children—meet their heavy task loads.

Whisky was also a principal product in many patent medicines. One such medicine is reported to have contained two ounces of Peruvian bark, half an ounce of Virginia snake root, and more than 50 ounces (3-1/2 pints) of whisky.[2]

Aside from the log cabins, the country was thickly dotted with other drinking places, in towns, villages and along the rough roads. In Lower Canada, there were twice as many bars and taverns as there were schools, Montreal's *Vindicator* reported on March 27, 1832. There were reported to be 1,892 "taverns [and] shops licensed to retail spirituous liquors" in the province, compared with 937 schools. That was said to mean a tavern or sales outlet "for every 128 persons of a fit age to indulge in Intemperance," compared with one school "for every 164 persons of a fit age to receive instruction." There were, said the *Vindicator,* 154,000 children "who ought to be in school," but only 45,000 who were.

Upper Canada seemed equally well supplied with drinking places. In 1833, there were 20 taverns on the 65-kilometre stage road between York and Hamilton. Bathurst District, in 1836, had 65 inns and 35 shops that sold, and usually served, liquor; London, with 1,300 people, had seven taverns.

"In travelling through the country, you will see every inn, tavern and beer shop filled at all hours with drunken, brawling fellows; and the quantity of ardent spirits consumed by them will truly astonish you," one anonymous "ex-settler" wrote.[3]

In many smaller villages and towns, taverns offered the only space large enough to accommodate even small crowds. They were used for weddings, funerals, meetings, elections, court proceedings (where juries were sometimes served whisky and even magistrate were known to imbibe while administering justice), and religious services.

Every event was an occasion for drinking whisky, but none more notoriously so than the "bees" or raisings at which log houses and barns were built. At one three-day raising, no more than 30 men were reported to have consumed 15 gallons of whisky—60 ounces of whisky per man.

Not every pioneer settler, of course, was a drunkard. The most successful were invariably moderate drinkers or teetotallers. And the first temperance movements were gathering forces by the 1830s. But heavy drinking would remain a costly social Canadian problem for decades.

(Endnotes)

1 M.A. Garland and J.S. Talman. *Pioneer Drinking Habits and the Rise of Temperance Agitation in Upper Canada Prior to 1840.* Ontario Historical Society, Papers and Records, volume 27 (1931), pp. 341-64.

2 Craig Heron. *Booze: A Distilled History.* Toronto: Between the Lines, 2003.

3 Garland and Talman, *Pioneer Drinking Habits.*

A house goes up as whisky goes down

William Thomson was unlike the troop of well-to-do, leisure class Britons who toured Canada in the early nineteenth century to write books about what they saw. A textile worker from the Aberdeen area of Scotland, Thomson supported himself during a three-year tour of the United States and Canada by working at whatever jobs he could find. One job was working at a "raising" of a log house in Vaughan Township, north of Toronto, "for a poor Irishman and his family." As the house went up, whisky went down. Following is an excerpt from *A Tradesman's Travels in the United States and Canada, in the Years 1840, 41 & 42,* Edinburgh, 1842.

Many accidents happen, and lives are frequently lost on these occasions, both from accidents and quarrels.

I was on the ground early and found the settler and his wife busy cooking at a large fire, surrounded by fallen trees and brushwood. The neighbours came by twos and threes, from different quarters, with axes over their shoulders; and as they came up each got a drink of whisky out of a tin can. The stuff smelled most horribly, yet none of them made a wry face of it...

At first they went to work moderately and with quietness, but after the whisky had been handed about several times, they got very uproarious—swearing, shouting, tumbling down, and sometimes like to fight. I then left off working, thinking I would be as safe out of the way a little; but this would not do, as they would have no idlers there. The handing round of the whisky was offered to me, but I declined the honour, being a teetotaller. So I had no choice but to commence working again, as I wished to see the end of the matter. I was sick of it before this; for most of them were drunk and all of them excited. The manner in which they used their axes was a "caution." Many accidents happen, and lives are frequently lost on these occasions, both from accidents and quarrels.

In all there were about 24 men, one half Irish; on the whole about the roughest specimens of humanity I have ever seen... The walls of a house, 15 by 26, and 12 feet high, were up before night, and some of the nearest neighbours were to return next day and cut out the doors and windows. When all was done they sat down, all about, eating bread and meat, and drinking whisky (I believe of the same quality as that known in Aberdeen by the name of *"Kill the carter")*.

Temperance groups wage holy war on booze

Curbed by a holy war waged by temperance advocates and teetotalers, Canada's nineteenth century booze epidemic peaked in the 1820s and 1830s. Hundreds of temperance societies sprang up within a few years. They were led mostly by Methodists, Baptists, Presbyterians and assorted Bible pounders, preaching salvation from the grip of life-destroying "ardent spirits." Largely standing on the sidelines—and sometimes in opposition to the teetotallers—were the two establishment churches, the Church of England (Anglican) and the Catholic Church of Rome.

The temperance warriors claimed great victories. Beyond doubt, they did much good. But they never achieved anything like a complete or lasting cure. The social curse remained a problem throughout at least the nineteenth century.

It was a war that would last almost a century, progressing through three phases: temperance, voluntary abstinence of all forms of booze, and law-enforced prohibition.

At first, the temperance societies were temperate in name and in fact. These were "societies of the temperate," advocating only

In the year after 120 workers at a lumber firm took the pledge, "no lives were lost, no limbs broken, and no serious accident is known to have occurred."

"abstaining from the use of distilled spirits," wrote the Rev. John Edgar, Belfast professor of divinity, in a lengthy lead article on "Principles and Objects of Temperance Societies," in the first issue of Montreal's *Canada Temperance Advocate,* May 1835. "The Christian," claimed Rev. Edgar, "is not forbidden the use of wine" and "does not consider the use of wine to be sinful." Temperance meant the temperate consumption of fermented alcohol.

Before long, however, most anti-booze organizations, except in Quebec, required the long pledge, total abstinence of all alcoholic beverages.

It was not without a fight that the aim of total abstinence prevailed. Women were champion advocators. "Lips that touch wine shall never touch mine," chimed the most chaste maidens. Some might well have become old maids, since the available supply of eligible, teetotalling males was rather limited. It was one thing for a man to swear off whisky. Thousands did, and some even managed to stay on the wagon. But for many, the thought of also giving up beer, wine, and cider, was a bridge too far.

The Anglican Church stood with opponents of the despised and ridiculed "cold water army," if for no other reason than their members were required to sip a little wine at communion service.

It was in the United States that the first temperance societies sprang up, in the early 1820s. The first two in Canada were organized in 1828, at Pictou, Nova Scotia, and in Montreal. Ross Duncan, Presbyterian minister and educator (he also farmed in order to feed his large family) founded the Pictou Society in January. Founders of the Montreal Temperance Society included Jacob De Witt, one of Lower Canada's most successful businessmen and financiers, a long-serving member of the House of Assembly, and an elder in the Presbyterian Church.

Upper Canada had 10,000 sworn teetotallers in 1832; Nova Scotia had 30,000 by 1837.

By 1832, according to historian Craig Heron, Upper Canada claimed 100 temperance societies with more than 10,000 members; Nova Scotia claimed 30,000 members by 1837.

Buckingham, in Lower Canada, was an example of the remarkable success claimed by temperance societies, according to a report in the May, 1835 premier issue of the *Canada Temperance Advocate*. The Buckingham society had been organized less than three years earlier, "under circumstances affording but slight prospect of success," the paper reported. Lumbering was the main industry, and employed some 150 men.

Booze was "considered indispensably necessary to protect against the cold and heat, and afford strength for the performance of the severe labour required." Despite this, the anti-booze preachers persuaded 120 men to take the pledge, and the lumbering firms stopped providing their workers with whisky. The result, it was said, was that lumbering had become much more productive without the former "riot, confusion and drunkenness." Better yet, in the preceding year "no lives were lost, no limbs were broken, and no serious accident is known to have occurred."

Despite the best efforts of the anti-boozers, teetotallers remained a minority and, although somewhat curbed, booze remained a nineteenth century problem, as evidenced by a few random reports.

•1845. Peterborough, with a population of 2,000, has no more than 150 temperance members but supports a brewery, three distilleries, and, with 20 licenced taverns, it had a ratio of one drinking place for every 100 men, women and children.

•1879. Winnipeg physicians claim that two-thirds of their male patients "suffer in some way or other from alcoholic poison," the *Winnipeg Tribune* reports April 15.

•1890. Canadians spent $38 million for 22 million gallons of spirits, wine and beer, and almost $800 million in the 25 years following Confederation, the Toronto *Farmer's Sun* reported, May 17, 1892. The 1890 consumption amounted to more than nine gallons per adult over age 19.

•1900. An advertisement in the Montreal

Family Herald and Weekly Sun, October 3, tells wives how to avoid "the disgrace, suffering, misery, and privation" resulting from their "husband's drinking habits." The secret is to sneak a little of the advertised patent medicine into his food and coffee.

•1904. Prime Minister John A. Macdonald notes that among the members of the Royal North West Mounted Police, "there is still a good deal of drinking," the *Winnipeg Free Press* reports, July 5.

•1919. Within about five years, prohibition has come and largely gone across Canada—except in Quebec, where prohibition lasted only a few months and prohibited only distilled liquor. The veterans are back from the Great War. Booze sales for the year included 4.8 million gallons of distilled liquor and 35 million gallons of beer—about eight gallons per adult, not counting wine or cider, according to Statistics Canada (*Historical Statistics of Canada, second edition,* 1983). The long-running U.S. prohibition followed immediately, on January 1, 1920. Production of Canadian whisky, and importation of Scotch, soared, to help slake the thirst of dry Americans.

Queen's University Archives

Reading the Proclamation of Canada, Market Square, Kingston, Ontario, July 1, 1868. Toronto celebrated with a roasted ox, but in Nova Scotia, a Father of Confederation was burned in effigy, together with a live rat.

Cheers and wailing greet July 1, 1867

As midnight broke on July 1, 1867, there was neither peace nor quiet across the land. From Halifax to Windsor, guns boomed, bells chimed, rifles, pistols and muskets were fired, bonfires were lit, as millions of Canadians poured out into the streets of towns and villages to celebrate the birth of their new country. Scant hours later, there were parades, military reviews, speeches, picnics, cricket and lacrosse matches, special railway and steamship excursions. In Toronto, a fat ox was roasted for the benefit of the poor, but in Nova Scotia an effigy of one of the Fathers of Confederation was burned together with a live rat.

The enthusiastic rejoicing on that first Canada Day when Nova Scotia, New Brunswick, Canada East and Canada West were officially forged into a new nation was not universally shared. For some in the two Maritime provinces there was bitter resentment at perceived loss of independence — and for some politicians, a loss of power and privileges.

In Canada East there were mixed feelings. Unionists saw Confederation as a bulwark against the threat of American annexation and the obliteration of French language, culture, customs, and institutions. Others feared that the British North America Act, the new constitution for the new country, gave too much power to the federal government, and not enough for Quebec to protect its interests.

From that first Confederation conference at Charlottetown in 1864, it had taken almost three years to put Canada together, and at times the whole idea was in danger of collapsing. The vision of a new nation from sea to sea to sea was far from complete. Prince Edward Island had opted out, and would stay out for another seven years. Newfoundland, too, had rejected Canada, and would not join for another 82 years. Manitoba, the Northwest Territories, and British Columbia were still to join the four million people of Canada.

Newspaper piss and vinegar

Less than two months before Dominion Day, the *British Colonist* and the *Acadian Recorder* had somewhat differing accounts of a Halifax meeting called to nominate candidates for the impending new Parliament.

The April 30 meeting "broke up in the wildest uproar and confusion," the anti-union *Acadian Recorder* reported the next day. The names of candidates were said to have been "called out amid great hissing,"

while "disgust and distrust seemed to be the leading elements which animated the breasts of the audience. 'Traitor' was called out in every quarter of the Hall." Confederation advocate Dr. Charles Tupper was said to have received "the loudest demonstration of disapproval," but when the name of anti-Confederation leader Joseph Howe was mentioned "a large majority of the audience arose and gave three hearty cheers for the Nova Scotia patriot."

A pack of "low and disgusting falsehoods" and "unblushing lies" was how the *British Colonist* described the *Acadian* report. Temperance Hall, said the union paper, was filled to capacity and hundreds had to be turned away. The "few obstructive" anti-unionists, in this report, "were silenced by the enthusiastic demonstrations of the mass of the friends of Union, whose rapturous plaudits cheered on the able and eloquent speakers." As for Dr. Tupper, far from being greeted with demonstrations of disapproval, he "was received with the wildest demonstrations of applause, and listened to with the most rapt attention." Other anti-unionists were accused of even worse, of "downright lying" and "odious, cowardly, unspeakable manners."

Cheers and boos

On Dominion Day itself, July 1, 1867, there was cheering across the continent, mixed with a few loud raspberries.

In Toronto, the *Leader* reported, "The New Dominion was hailed last night as the clock struck twelve by Mr. Rawlinson ringing a merry peel on the joy bells of St. James Cathedral... The bells had scarcely commenced when the firing of small arms was heard in every direction, so that both music and gunpowder were brought into requisition to usher in the great event. Large bonfires were lighted on various parts of the city... Large crowds also paraded the streets with fifes and drums, cheering in the heartiest manner."

Great events were scheduled to start at the crack of dawn. All the troops in the city were to parade to the review grounds where they were to be "supplied with ale at the expense of Mr. Gzowski [Sir Casimir, former superintendent of public works]. In the evening there were to be military bands, fireworks and Chinese lanterns at Queen's Park; "a picnic and festival" on the government grounds, while "A fat ox will be roasted and given away to the poor... by Capt. Woodhouse, of the schooner *Lord Nelson*." An event held at the city's Crystal Palace was characterized by the *Leader* as "a loathing band of so-called mothers exhibiting their offspring for prizes—a horrid and disgusting exhibition."

In Peterborough, on the northern flank of Ontario settlement, midnight bell ringing "was a cause of alarm" to many citizens, according to the *Examiner*. "But very soon they found their fears were groundless; the cause was nothing more than introducing our citizens to Confederation."

In Ottawa, thousands gathered as a match was struck at midnight to ignite a huge bonfire, all the city bells rang out, rockets flared,

Up to Canada to determine if British principles are to "flourish... or unbridled democracy shall have a whole continent on which to erect the despotism of the mob."

and 100 guns of the Ottawa field battery boomed, the *Citizen* reported on July 4. There must have been little sleep for the players and spectators of four lacrosse games that started at 7 a.m. At the new Parliament Buildings, spectators and an honour guard awaited the arrival of the cabinet headed by John A. Macdonald, a gaggle of dignitaries, and Charles Monck, for his installation as Canada's first Governor General.

Confederation, predicted the *Ottawa Times* that day, will solve "a great problem" with which "the whole world is intimately concerned —whether British constitutional principles are to take root and flourish on the Western Hemisphere, or unbridled Democracy shall have a whole continent on which to erect the despotism of the mob. The issue is one of national existence combined with the enjoyment of national liberty, against the universal rule of an unrestrained Democracy."

In Quebec, the *Journal des Trois Rivieres* viewed the bells and guns as a proud announcement that "we have taken our place among the nations of the earth."

Montreal greeted July 1 at 4 a.m. when the guns of the Montreal Field Battery "boomed forth a royal salute," followed two hours later by more salutes from the guns at St. Helen's Island. The *Gazette* called it "the greatest day in the history of the North American province since Jacques Cartier landed at Stadacona."

Far away from the new Dominion, at the

tip of Vancouver Island, Victoria's *Daily Colonist* greeted July 1 as a "memorable day for British North America." Its publisher, Amor de Cosmos, was apparently breaking with his long-time mentor Joseph Howe. Canada, de Cosmos predicted, will "play an important part in the world's history," guided by "a ministry composed of the best and greatest minds on the continent." Confederation had "given the deathblow to Annexation." All that remained to make the country complete was the construction of a railway to the Pacific coast and the admission of British Columbia into confederation "as rapidly as possible."

Mourning in the Maritimes
In Nova Scotia and New Brunswick, there were a few muted cheers and some loud sobbing.

In Halifax, the *British Colonist* greeted the day with a rambling headline: "DOMINION DAY. UNIVERSAL REJOICING. Gorgeous Decorations. Enthusiastic Celebration of the Inauguration of the Dominion of Canada. Grand Display of Fireworks. Illumination, Bon Fires, &c. NAVAL AND MILITARY REVIEW."

The *Morning Chronicle* published an obituary.

"DIED.

"Last night, at twelve o'clock, the free and enlightened Province of Nova Scotia. Deceased was the offspring of Old English stock, and promised to have proved an honour and support to her parents in their declining years. Her death was occasioned by unnatural treatment received at the hands of some of her ungrateful sons, who, taking advantage of the position she afforded them, betrayed her to the enemy. Funeral will take place from the Grande Parade this day, Monday, at 9 o'clock. Friends are requested not to attend, as her enemies, with becoming scorn, intend to insult the occasion with rejoicing."

In Saint John, "There was nothing uproarious about the demonstrations" that marked July 1, the *Morning News* reported. "Everything was conducted in an orderly and becoming spirit, gratifying to the friends of the Union and at the same time not calculated to create an undue feeling of unpleasantness in the minds of those who have opposed the measure from a conviction of its unsuitability for our people."

According to Timothy Anglin's *Morning Freeman,* some of those politicians who had sought union for their own aggrandizement were rewarded, and some were disappointed. While Confederation Fathers James Mitchell and Leonard Tilley got cabinet posts "with salaries and pickings worth $8,000 to $10,000 per year," "poor Dr. Tupper had to relinquish all idea of taking immediate possession of the seat in the cabinet of the new Dominion which was the prize he so coveted that he sold his country for the chance of winning it."

Elsewhere in Nova Scotia, July 1 was "by no means a day of rejoicing," in the view of the *Yarmouth Herald.* "There was a burlesque celebration in the morning," but numerous flags were reportedly flown at half-mast. "In several localities men wore black weeds on their hats," while at Milton, an effigy of Tupper "was suspended by the neck all afternoon" and in the evening "burnt side by side with a live rat."

World's leading multicultural nation

Canadian multiculturalism became official on October 8, 1971, when Liberal Prime Minister Pierre Trudeau announced a "Policy of Multiculturalism Within a Bilingual Framework" in the House of Commons. It was entrenched in the constitution in 1982 with the declaration in the Charter of Rights and Freedoms' that all Canadians are equal before the law, "without discrimination." It was further cemented in law in 1988 under the Progressive Conservative government of Brian Mulroney, with the passage of the *Canadian Multicultural Act.*

Thus did Canada become the only country to entrench multiculturalism in its constitution and laws.

The world's highest per capita immigration rate has made this country one of the world's most racial and ethnically diverse—and peaceful. It has been hailed as a "model for the world."

It is a diversity that is driven by necessity. Without immigration, Canada would have a shrinking population and tough economic problems. We would have a diminishing workforce to support an increasing number of increasingly aged seniors. Immigrants are needed to avert that by maintaining an adequate number of working, earning and tax-paying Canadians.

Strangers at our gates

In reality, Canada was a multicultural nation long before the fact was recognized and celebrated.

In its first three decades as a confederated nation, Canada was populated almost entirely by English-, French- and native-speaking peoples. That changed at the start of the twentieth century when the Canadian Pacific Railway opened the West for settlement, and millions of immigrants arrived. Population increased 50 percent in the first 15 years of the century, from 5.3 million to 7.9 million people. Most of the arrivals came from such European counties as the Ukraine, Poland, Germany, and Austria. Many knew neither English nor French.

They were Immigration Minister Clifford Sifton's "men in sheepskin clothing," peasant settlers brought here to turn prairie sod into wheat fields. It was the start of Canada's multicultural mosaic.

They were not that warmly welcomed by the prairie British—the English, Scots, Welsh and Irish. Among the first of the Ukrainian settlers to arrive in Saskatchewan were the parents of Paul Yuzyk, who was born 1903, 10 years after his father arrived. After graduating with top marks from the province's teaching college, he was rejected for 77 advertised teaching positions, by local school boards who didn't want "foreigners" teaching their British students. "We were being called bohunks and foreigners," Yuzyk later recalled. "I said to myself that if they called me a foreigner when I had been born in Canada, it meant Canada needed some changing." His efforts to do just that would later earn him the unofficial title of Canada's "Father of multiculturalism."

Taunts of "foreigner," "bohunk," and worse were still ringing in the prairie air when a Scot took up the multiculturalism cause. John Buchan, historian, scholar, diplomat and novelist, was best known for his espionage thriller novel and movie, *The 39 Steps*. As Baron Tweedsmuir, he was Canada's governor general from late 1935 until his death in early 1940. He was the first to be chosen by Canada, and one of the last non-Canadian governors general. For more

> "If they called me a foreigner when I had been born here, it meant that Canada needed some changing."

than four years, he beat the drums for multiculturalism, in speeches, radio addresses, and news media interviews.

"It is the glory of our empire to embrace within its confines many races and traditions," Buchan told parliamentarians and assembled dignitaries at his installation at Quebec City. "It is in variety that strength lies."

Three weeks later (November 28) he urged Canada's ethnic groups to "retain their individuality and each make its contribution to the national character," in a speech to a joint meeting of the Canadian and Empire clubs in Toronto. Each ethnic group, he said, should learn "from the other, and that while they cherish their own special loyalties and traditions, they cherish not less that new loyalty and tradition which springs from their union."

In Fraserwood, Manitoba, September 1936, he told a large crowd of Ukrainian Canadians: "You will all be better Canadians for being also good Ukrainians… The strongest nations are those that are made up of different racial elements."

"In radio addresses and speaking tours across the country, he encouraged groups to keep their 'authentic,' 'racial' identities: Icelanders in Gimli, Acadians in Annapolis Royal, Québécois in Montreal, Scots in Ontario," author and journalist Doug Saunders writes.[1]

Buchan was the most popular, energetic, scholarly, and liberal of the long line of British governors general. His death in Feb-

The historic Ottawa home of the Global Centre for Pluralism. The section on the right was built in 1923 to house the Dominion Archives; the left wing was added when the site became the Canadian War Museum. The building was leased from the federal government by Pluralism in late 2011 and, after renovations, will be occuppied by the Centre in 2014.

ruary 1940, during his term in office, was marked by a state funeral in Ottawa before his ashes were returned to Scotland.

The father of multiculturalism

Skip twenty-four years to Ottawa, March 3, 1964 and the Senate's Red Chamber. Paul Yuzyk is now a professor at the University of Manitoba, historian, author, a leader of the prairie Ukrainian-Canadians, and a newly-minted senator, appointed by his longtime Saskatchewan friend, Prime Minister Diefenbaker, shortly before the election of Lester Pearson's Liberal government.

Yuzyk is about to make his maiden Senatorial speech, and he has a bee in his bonnet. Eight months earlier, Pearson appointed the Royal Commission on Bilingualism and Biculturalism to inquire into the status of these two perceived foundations of Can-

ada. After attacking biculturalism as a slight to the millions of Canadians who are of neither British nor French descent, Yuzyk delivers the heart of his message:

"The Indians and Eskimos have been with us throughout our history; the British group is multicultural—English, Scots, Irish, Welsh; and with the setting up of other ethnic groups, which now make up almost a third of the population, Canada has become multicultural in fact ... In keeping with the ideals of democracy and the spirit of Confederation, Canada should accept and guarantee the principle of the partnership of all peoples who have contributed to her development and progress."

It was perhaps the apex of Yuzyk's campaign for multicultural recognition. Seven years later, when Trudeau declared, "Cultural pluralism is the very essence of Canadian identity" and made multiculturalism official, the new policy was greeted with enthusiasm by the opposition parties. This "excellent declaration" is "most welcome," said Opposition Leader Robert Stanfield. Crediste leader Real Caoutte hailed it as recognition that Canada is "one nation" with two official languages and a "multiplicity of colours." But when he died in 1986, it was Paul Yuzyk who was hailed by the *Ukrainian Weekly* as "the father of multiculturalism."

Diversity increasingly diverse

The number and proportion of Canadians of other than British or French heritage is not only increasing with immigration, it is becoming increasingly diverse.

On the heels of the Second World War, millions of immigrants from Europe—especially from Germany and Italy—settled here. But in the final decades of the twentieth and into the twenty-first century, most of the newcomers came from Asia.

By the time of the 2001 census, Canada had 30 ethnic groups with at least 100,000 members each, and 10 ethnic groups with more than one million each. British and French descendents were barely more than half the total. Other major ethnic groups were Germans, 10 percent of the total population; Italians, 4.6 percent; South Asians and aboriginal people, 4 percent each; and Chinese, 3.9 percent.

In 2010, some 280,000 permanent im-

"Canada is today the most successful pluralist society on the face of the globe."

migrants arrived, of which fewer than 14 percent claimed either English (26,000) or French (10,000) as their mother tongue, Citizenship and Immigration reported in its *Facts and Figures 2010*. Tagalog was the most widely spoken mother tongue. At 34,000 it exceeded the number of immigrants who claimed either English or French as their mother tongue. Almost one quarter of the immigrants (74,000) were classed as having neither English nor French language ability.

As long as a high level of immigration is maintained, Canada seems certain to retain a rich variety of heritages. But as different cultures mingle and marry over generations, traditional identities blur, and "Canadian" emerges as the largest. What, for example, can you call a person with, say, Cree or Assiniboine, Scottish, French and Italian heritage, other than Canadian? In the 2006 census, nearly 5.8 million respondents identified "Canadian" as their only ethnic or cultural origin, far more than any other group.

Global stature

The person who has probably done more than any other to raise the global stature of Canada's multiculturalism is Prince Karim Aga Khan IV, philanthropist, and spiritual leader (Imam) of the world's 15 million and Canada's 45,000 Shia Ismaili Muslims, known in Canada for their entrepreneurial skills. The Harvard-educated Aga Khan's full time job appears to be as head of the non-profit Aga Khan Development Network, which claims to be "the world's largest, private international development network," with an annual budget of some $2 billion.

"Canada is today the most successful pluralist society on the face of the globe, without a doubt in my mind," the Aga Khan told the *Globe and Mail*, February 2, 2002. "That is something unique to Canada. It is an amazing global human asset," and a model for those world regions that are burdened by "The inability of different groups to live together in peace in a constructive environment and build a civil society."

The Aga Khan was not in Ottawa just to make press statements. He had come to establish the Global Centre for Pluralism, with a mission "to promote pluralist values and practices in culturally diverse societies worldwide to ensure that every individual has the opportunity to realize his or her full potential as a citizen, irrespective of cultural, ethnic or religious differences."

So politically appealing was the concept of such a centre that both Liberal Prime Minister Paul Martin and Conservative Prime Minister Stephen Harper sought credit for the government's participation with the Aga Khan Development Network in funding the new think tank.

On April 15, 2005, Paul Martin's government announced that it "intends to contribute $30 million" to the endowment of the new centre, with $40 million to come from the Aga Khan Development Network.

The global centre "will provide important support for our continued efforts to foster democracy and good governance in the world," Martin stated.

Less than nine months later, the Martin government is defeated in the 2006 national elections and on October 26, it is Stephen Harper's turn to announce that "Canada's new government joins with the Aga Khan to create the Global Centre for Pluralism," with the same $30 million in government support promised by Martin.

By late 2011, the Global Centre for Pluralism had assembled an eleven-person board of directors that includes such notables as former UN Secretary General Kofi Annan and former Governor General Adrienne Clarkson; appointed Canadian diplomat John McNee as its first secretary-general, and was spending $20 million to rehabilitate an idle national historic site that will be its new headquarters. Originally built to house Canada's first national archives in 1906, the building at 230 Sussex Drive—sandwiched between the Royal Canadian Mint, the National Art Gallery, and the Ottawa River—sprouted wings to triple in size and become the Canadian War Museum in 1986. It languished empty after 2005 when the War Museum moved to its vastly greater, new facilities, until Pluralism leased it from the government.

(Endnotes)
1 Three lies Canada tells about itself. http://dougsaunders.tumblr.com/post/4370993762/the-three-lies-canada-tells-about-itself (2011.10.31.

A world leader

In the advance of human rights and envi ronmental protection, Canada was a world leader in the second half of the twentieth century. The 1948 UN Declaration of Human Rights, the creation of NATO, the Rights of the Child, and the International Criminal Court are a few of the global landmarks in which Canada played a major— sometimes *the* major—role.

The father of NATO
1948 April 29. Louis St.Laurent (external afairs minister and future prime minister) in the House of Commons, proposes a "collective security league." This soon became NATO (North American Atlantic Treaty Organization) in which Canada, the United States, and Western European nations pledged mutual defence in the event of a Soviet attack. After the Cold War, NATO forces played a vital role in such actions as quelling the civil war that followed the breakup of the former Yugoslavia, and assisting in overthrowing Gadhafi's Libyan reign of tyranny and terrorism in 2011.

Universal rights
1948 December 8. The Universal Declaration of Human Rights, authored principally by Canadian diplomat John Peters Humphrey, adopted by UN General Assembly (see separate feature).

Canada invents peacekeeping
1956 November 7. With the authorization of an Emergency Force in response to the Suez Crisis, the United Nations adopts a concept of multinational peacekeeping forces under UN command, advocated by Canada's External Affairs Minister and future Prime Minister Lester Pearson (1897-1972). France, Britain and Israel invaded Egypt after Egyptian military ruler Gamel Abdel Nasser nationalized the Suez Canal. Pressure by the United Nations, the United States and the Soviet Union forced withdrawal of the invading forces. Troops from five countries were sent to keep the peace. Troops from six more countries later joined this first UN peacekeeping force. The peacekeepers remained in Egypt for more than a decade. Pearson won the Nobel Peace Prize in 1957 for having "saved the world," according to the Nobel citation. Another Nobel Peace Prize was awarded in 1988 to UN Peacekeeping forces as a whole. By 2011,

UN peacekeepers had been sent on 63 missions around the world, with Canadian forces among the most prominent participants.

Saving lives from ultraviolet light
1987 September 15. The Montreal Protocol *to Reduce Substances that Deplete the Ozone Layer,* a Canadian initiative, is signed by diplomats from 40 countries and later ratified by 191. The ozone layer protects the earth from harmful ultraviolet light. A sharp depletion of this protective layer in the upper atmosphere threatened human health, causing, among other things, increases in skin cancer and cataracts, as well as threatening other forms of animal and plant life. The principal depleting substance is chlorofluorocarbons (CFCs), used in refrigerators, aerosol spays and other products. Success of the Montreal Protocol was "nothing less than spectacular," the UN reported 20 years after the signing. The 191 nations had "reduced their consumption of ozone-depleting substances by approximately 95 percent."

Rights of the child
1990 September 2. The UN Convention on The Rights of the Child—instigated and promoted principally by Prime Minister Brian Mulroney—becomes international law with the required minimum ratification by 20 UN counties. By 1993 it had been ratified by more countries than any other UN convention, all but two of the UN member states. The exceptions were Somalia and the United States. The convention sets out civil, political, economic, social, health and cultural rights of persons under age 18.

Library and Archives Canada e002505448

Lester Pearson won the Nobel Peace Prize in 1957 for creating UN peacekeeping forces.

International criminal court
1998 July 17. Lead by Canada, a Rome conference approves a treaty for the International Criminal Court, to investigate and prosecute war crimes, crimes against humanity, and genocide (see page 128).

Responsibility to protect
2006 April 28. UN Security Council authorizes the "responsibility-to-protect" principle, the Canadian-led initiative that asserts that the international responsibility to protect civilians overrides the rights of national sovereignty (see page 133).

Canada's father of modern human rights

Three-and-a-half years after the founding of the United Nations in San Francisco, the nations of the world met in General Assembly in Paris to lay a foundation stone, *The Universal Declaration of Human Rights (UDHR)*. It is "the international Magna Carta of all mankind," in the words of U.S. First Lady Eleanor Roosevelt. "One of humanity's most shining achievements," in the words of UN High Commissioner for Human Rights Navanethem Pillay. The principal drafter of this 30-article document was a Canadian lawyer, professor and human rights advocate, John Peters Humphrey, "the father of the modern human rights system," in the words of Nelson Mandela.

Born in the small New Brunswick town of Hampton, as a young child Humphrey lost both his parents to cancer and an arm to an accident while playing with fire; endured a boarding school education; enrolled in Mount Allison University at age 15; moved to Montreal and McGill University, where he earned degrees in commerce, arts, and law, with a Master's in international law. He conducted a brief law practice in Montreal, before accepting a teaching post at McGill.

At McGill in the early 1940s, Humphrey met Henri Laugier, a Second World War refugee from German-occupied France who had worked for the Free French. When the British liberated North Africa, Laugier moved to Algeria to teach at the University of Algiers. Five weeks after Germany's surrender ended the war in Europe in May, 1945, 51 founding nations signed the UN Charter in San Francisco. The UN's first assistant secretary-general was Laugier. In 1946, Laugier hired Humphrey as the first director of the UN's Division of Human Rights, a position he held for 20 years.

A UN Commission on Human Rights was formed, with Eleanor Roosevelt as chair, to prepare what was initially conceived as an International Bill of Rights, but would emerge as the Universal Declaration of Human Rights. The rights in the declaration had to be acceptable to the varying racial, cultural and religious tenets of the commission members, from Australia, Belgium, Byelorussia, Chile, China, Egypt, France, India, Iran, Lebanon, Panama, Philippines, United Kingdom, United States, Soviet Union, Uruguay and Yugoslavia. No small challenge.

While the rights had to be universal, the idea was not. "Any attempt by the United Nations to formulate a Declaration of Human Rights in individualistic terms would quite inevitably fail," Harold Laski, considered one of the great political scientists of his time, predicted. Even the government of Canada was initially opposed, much to Humphrey's chagrin. Numerous objectors believed that an "attempt to reach a consensus on rights would only promote conflict and incite the kind of vapid moralizing which the Ottawa men disliked," Humphrey wrote.

It was in the face of this doubt and opposition that Humphrey tackled the task of preparing a draft declaration. His 408-page document was the basis on which, after two years of much debate, the Universal Declaration was adopted by the UN General Assembly in Paris on December 8, 1948. December 8 is still observed in most of the world as Human Rights Day.

"The UDHR and the forces of moderation, tolerance and understanding that the text represents will probably in future history-writing be seen as one of the greatest steps forward in the process of global civilization," Asbjorn Eide, founder of the Norwegian Institute of Human Rights at the University of Oslo, wrote in 1992.

But Humphrey was not satisfied. "Human rights without economic and social rights have little meaning for most people, particularly on empty bellies," he wrote. It was an echo of one of Franklin D. Roosevelt's famous four freedoms, "free-

Photo courtesy John Peters Humphrey Foundation.

John Peters Humphrey, "The father of the modern human rights system," in the words of Nelson Mandela.

dom from want." The UN addressed this concern in 1966 with the adoption of the International Covenant on Economic, Social and Cultural Rights, together with the Covenant on Civil and Political Rights. These two covenants and the UDHR now comprise the UN's International Bill of Human Rights.

The lofty goals of the UDHR are manifestly far from achieved. Billions of people are still deprived of the declared basic rights. Yet more people than ever now live with the freedom of those rights. And UDHR is a crucial instrument for the protection and promotion of those rights. It has been incorporated in the constitutions of more than one hundred counties; dozens of legally binding international treaties are based on its principles; and it has been cited as justification for numerous UN activities.

Perhaps the most powerful tool for establishing the rights espoused by the UDR will prove to be the International Criminal Court, charged with prosecuting perpetrators of genocide, crimes against humanity, and war crimes—another Canadian initiative.

During his term as UN Director of Human Rights, Humphrey guided the implementation of 67 international covenants as well as new constitutions for scores of countries; promoted press freedom and the status of women; fought racial discrimination; and proposed creation of the office of UN High Commissioner for Human Rights. He received the UN Human Rights Award in 1988, on the fortieth anniversary of the Declaration of Human Rights.

Humphrey returned to McGill University in 1966, where he taught while continuing to promote human rights in Canada and abroad until his retirement at age 89, the year before his death.

Global meeting awaits fate of International Criminal Court

It is Friday evening, July 17, 1998. More than 300 people, crammed into the Red Room of the United Nation's Food and Agriculture building in Rome, are gripped by anticipation and apprehension. They include delegates representing 148 countries, their advisors and assistants, United Nations officials, and a large phalanx representing some 800 non-governmental organizations (NGO) from across the globe. The conference has been underway for almost five weeks. The "plenipotentiaries"—the government delegates with signing authority—joined it two days ago. Now, within the next few hours, they must decide the fate of a proposed International Criminal Court. Its mission is to investigate and prosecute people accused of war crimes, crimes against humanity, or genocide.

In continuous negotiations since the start of the conference, a Preliminary Commission sought agreement on a text that, hopefully, the plenipotentiaries could approve and sign within the final three days of the conference. The Commission worked with the text of a treaty that had evolved during eight preceding years of drafting and negotiating.

The crowded meeting in the Red Room to determine the fate of the latest version of this long hashed-over text would climax—one way or another—almost a century-and-half of ill-fated proposals for some form of an international criminal court.

An ill-fated history
Gustav Moynier, one of the Red Cross founders, may have been the first to issue a public call for an international court to deal with major atrocities. In 1872 Moynier issued a proposal for a court to prosecute perpetrators of crimes committed during the Franco-Prussian war. In 1919, delegates at the Paris Peace conference proposed a court to try the German Kaiser and others for crimes of the First World War. In 1937, member states of the League of Nations signed a treaty for an international criminal court, but it failed when few nations ratified it. In 1947, on the heels of the Second

World War, the UN General Assembly asked its International Law Commission to draft a court-establishing treaty. Completed in 1953, the proposed treaty dealt with crimes against peace, war crimes, crimes against humanity, and genocide. Caught in the Cold War, this treaty, too, failed to gain ratification. In 1975, Benjamin B. Ferenz, one of the chief U.S. prosecutors of Second World War criminals brought before the Nuremberg trials, issued a call for an international criminal court in his book *Defining International Aggression: The Search for World Peace.* The book attracted wide interest, but little action.

The text that the Rome conference set out to negotiate, revise and approve was initiated in 1991 when the UN General Assembly asked the International Law Commission to prepare yet another draft treaty. Completed in 1994, this latest ILC text was followed by four more years of negotiations and revisions by two international committees, involving hundreds of diplomats, UN officials, advisors, and NGO members.

Attracted by the UN initiative, some 200 NGOs in 1993 established a Coalition for an International Criminal Court. For three years, this NGO coalition joined governments and UN officials in discussions that sought agreement on revisions to this latest ILC draft. The NGO coalition members acted almost like non-voting members of the committees that did the negotiating. While the coalition worked at the UN level, the NGO organizations worked in their home countries to raise public and political awareness and support. The coalition eventually grew to some 800 NGOs.[1] Prominent members included Amnesty International, Human Rights Watch, and the World Federation Movement.

Canada was among those counties that wanted an independent court that would be free from control by the 15-member UN Security Council (with veto powers held by five countries) as well as free from restraint by individual countries. A group of a dozen like-minded countries "under the leadership of Canada and Norway... worked through the three years of negotiations as champions of a strong, independent and effective international court," two members of the NGO coalition later wrote. "They developed a strong partnership with the NGO coalition and with other experts, and their achievements were impressive."[2] This "Like-Minded Group" eventually expanded to embrace 60 countries. Its meetings were chaired by Canada, mostly by Montreal lawyer Philippe Kirsch, legal advisor to Canada's UN mission, a diplomat with extensive experience in international criminal law.

Canada also helped fund the NGO coalition, contributed to a UN fund to enable lesser developed countries to participate in the years of negotiations, and sought to increase public awareness and support of the proposed court.

The need for such a court was highlighted in 1994 by the creation of two ad hoc tribunals to try crimes of genocide in Rwanda and war crimes in the former Yugoslavia. For four years, Canadian Judge Louise Arbour was the chief prosecutor for the International Criminal Tribunal for the former Yugoslavia and initially for the

Rwanda tribunal. She indicted Yugoslav President Slobodan Milosevic for war crimes, the first serving head of state to be held to account before an international court. (Before his trial ended, Milosevic died while in prison.)

The final hurdle at Rome

Philippe Kirsch chaired the Rome conference commission tasked with the final negotiating work. His large contingent, almost the entire conference, had five weeks to revise and find agreement on this old, long hashed-over text.

Kirsch was described as "Pushy in driving delegations through negotiations… strong, determined, compelling and straightforward… NGO leaders all deeply trusted him."[3]

Perhaps so. But "The task awaiting the negotiators was daunting," Kirsch later wrote.[4] While a great deal had been accomplished, the lengthy text (more than 20,000 words) was still "riddled with some fourteen hundred… points of disagreement" and "any number of alternative texts. Within the time available, the conference could not possibly have resolved the outstanding issues systematically."

Outstanding issues included demands to expand the treaty to include crimes of aggression, trafficking in drugs, and terrorism, as well as specifying the use of nuclear weapons and land mines as war crimes. Who would control the court was a major issue.

A plethora of sub-committees and working groups met seven days a week. As time began to run out, the meetings lasted "most of the nights." Yet after three weeks of intense negotiations, progress toward agreement "had ground to a near standstill… The road to an acceptable text was neither certain nor apparent," Kirsch wrote in his account of the negotiating process.

Canada's Foreign Affairs Minister Lloyd Axworthy was one of the keynote speakers when the plenipotentiaries assembled on July 15. By prosecuting those who commit war crimes and genocide, the court "will help to end cycles of impunity and retribution," Axworthy told the delegates. "Without justice, there is no reconciliation, and without reconciliation, no peace." The court, he said, should have a "constructive relationship with the United Nations, but must be independent, able to initiate proceedings without having court jurisdiction 'triggered' only by a State complaint or a Security Council referral."[5]

Even as Axworthy spoke, with less than three days left to sign a treaty, there was still "no agreement on… the fundamental questions," Kirsch's account noted. The pushing by Kirsch and the lobbying of delegations by UN Secretary General Kofi Annan had failed to achieve a breakthrough. Kirsch was faced with two alternatives. He could report that no agreement had been reached, and suggest yet another effort at yet another, later conference. Or he and his "bureau of co-ordinates" could draft yet one more revised text, "designed to attract the broadest possible support."[6]

The first alternative seemed to offer little hope for success in the foreseeable future. And no one expected that a revised text would, at this late date, win the agreement of all the delegations. But there was hope that a revised, new text would attract enough delegates to sign the treaty and launch the court. The revised text was prepared with the burning of more midnight oil.

That is why, on the evening of Friday, July 17, those crowded into the Red Room in Rome were gripped by anticipation and apprehension as they considered Kirsch's new text and the fate of the International Criminal Court.

The first test came on a motion by India seeking amendments. Approval of these, it was argued, would sound the death knell of the treaty. The proposed amendments were defeated by a vote of 114 to 34. When a second set of amendments proposed by the United States was defeated by a similar margin, there was "cheering, hugging, weeping and rhythmetic applause."[7] The final test came just minutes before midnight, on another U.S. proposal, to reject the entire treaty. Instead, the treaty was approved by 120 states, with seven opposed and 21 abstaining. Those voting with the United States were Israel, China, Iraq, Yemen, Libya, and Qatar.

There was "hostility that lingers toward the United States, in countries that made hard concessions at Rome, only to see America reject the entire treaty."

At the treaty signing ceremonies on Saturday, Kofi Annan summed up what seemed to be the prevailing attitude of the court's strongest supporters:

"No doubt many of us would have liked a Court vested with even more far reaching powers, but that should not lead us to minimize the breakthrough you have achieved. The establishment of the court is still a gift of hope to future generations, and a giant step forward in the march towards universal human rights and the rule of law. It is an achievement which, only a few years ago, nobody would have thought possible."[8]

The United States missed an opportunity "to shape the court in America's image," Yale University law professor Ruth Wedgwood, wrote in a U.S. perspective of the Rome conference. President Bill Clinton and Foreign Secretary Madeleine Albright had touted the court "as a key aim of American foreign policy," but on terms considered necessary to U.S. interests. The United States missed its opportunity, Wedgwood wrote, because Washington failed to instruct its negotiators at Rome about the terms it would accept, until after three weeks of negotiations. By then it was too late to effectively argue the U.S case, according to Wedgewood.[9]

The United States was concerned that its troops, stationed across the world, "should not face the added danger of politically motivated prosecutions" because of an international court, Wedgwood argued. But at the same time, "Important changes were made in the draft treaty to reassure the United States." The result was "hostility that lingers toward the United States, in countries that made hard concession at Rome, only then to see America reject the entire treaty."

The treaty came into effect in 2002 when the required minimum 60 states had ratified it. It was another year before the court was up and running, with its headquarters in The Hague, Netherlands. Kirsch was among the first 18 elected judges, and served as the court's first president for more than six years. By 2012, the treaty had been ratified by 119 nations, who were thus the International Criminal Court's "state parties." The United States was still not among them.

(Endnotes)

1 Benedetti, Fanny and John L. Washburn. "Drafting the International Criminal Court Treaty: Two Years to Rome and an Afterword on the Rome Diplomatic Conference." *Global Governance,* v.5, no.1 (Jasnuary-March, 1999).

2 Ibid.

3 Ibid.

4 Kirsch, Philippe and John T. Holmes. "The Rome Conference on an International Criminal Court: The Negotiating Process." *American Journal of International Law.* V. 93, no. 1 (January 1999).

5 United Nations, *Diplomatic Conerence Begins Four Days of General Statements on Establishment of International Criminal Court.* Press Release L/ROM/7, http://www.un.org/icc/pressrel/lrom7.htm. Retrieved 20 November 2011.

6 Kirsch and Holmes.

7 Benedetti and Washburn.

8 Annan, Kofi, Speeches/Statements, United Nations. http://www.un.org/icc/speeches/718sg.htm Retrieved 20 November 2011.

9 Wedgwood, Ruth. "Fiddling in Rome: America and the International Criminal Court." *Foreign Affairs,* v.77, no. 6 (November-December 1998).

Lives trump sovereignty in Canadian doctrine

The United Nation's *Responsibility to Protect* (R2P) doctrine is a second Canadian-fashioned nail for the coffin of brutal dictators who rule with force to oppress, imprison, torture and kill their people. The International Criminal Court was the first. These initiatives are really two arms—and two arms can work better than one.

The struggle against oppression is as old as civilization and it has no end in sight. And R2P has met with both some success (in Libya) and abject failure (in Syria).

Lloyd Axworthy, Canada's foreign affairs minister from 1996 to 2001 led the effort to establish R2P. He was troubled by a feature of the UN charter, intended to prevent wars between nations by protecting national sovereignty. But this was also held as a shield to prevent UN intervention in the internal affairs of sovereign nations, and thus stop the UN from acting to avert such catastrophes as the 800,000 deaths in the 1994 Rwanda massacre and later ethnic cleansing in the Balkans.

At a New York news conference Thursday morning, September 14, 2000, Axworthy announced the creation of an International Commission on Intervention and State Sovereignty (ICISS). Its purpose, he said, was "to ensure that the indifference of the international community in the face of such situations as occurred in Rwanda and Srebrenica are no longer an option."

In a speech to the UN General Assembly that afternoon, Axworthy criticized the UN for "rigid notions of national sovereignty and narrow conception of national interests." He said the UN "remains increasingly inward-looking and driven by their own interests rather than by those of the ones they were designed to serve."

Opposition remained. For governments and autocrats alike, national sovereignty is a bulwark against foreign interference. At a London meeting of the ICISS in February, 2001 some useful diplomatic euphemisms were suggested by Michael Ignatieff, journalist, historian and future leader of Canada's Liberal Party. Instead of seeking the "right to intervene," or "obligation to intervene," Ignatief suggested the phase "responsibility to protect." In December, the ICISS issued its report, *The Responsibility to Protect*.

The UN General Assembly endorsed the doctrine in 2005 followed by the Security Council in 2006. "Each individual State has the responsibility to protect its populations from genocide, war crimes, ethnic cleansing, and crimes against humanity," the doctrine states. It adds: "The international community, through the United Nations, also has the responsibility to use appropriate diplomatic, humanitarian and other peaceful means" to help protect. But force remains a last resort: "…we are prepared to take collective action… should peaceful means be inadequate and national authorities manifestly fail to protect their populations."

Collective action followed a March 17, 2011 Security Council resolution that authorized "all necessary measures" short of invasion and occupation to protect Libya's civilians from Col. Gadhafi's forces, which had attacked peaceful demonstrations for democracy, and threatened a civilian massacre. American, French, British and Canadian missiles and aircraft began attacking Libyan military facilities and forces within two days.

This first military intervention under the *Responsibility to Protect* doctrine is generally deemed a success, although not without controversy. With the air and naval support of the coalition, the rebels overthrew the Gadhafi regime in seven months of fighting. The cost included an estimated 2,000 to 2,500 killed and a much greater number seriously wounded.

Gadhafi avoided trial by the International Criminal Court when he was shot and killed while trying to escape. Gadhafi's former spy chief, Abdullah al-Senussi, was arrested in Mauritania on March 11, 2012, almost precisely one year after the start of the collective action. The International Criminal Court, Libya, and France made competing claims for his extradition and trial. In September, al-Senussi was extradicted to Tripoli for trial. The London *Guardian* called the extradition "a blow to international justice, claiming that "one of the worst men left in the world" should be tried by the International Criminal Court.

If Libya was a success, R2P was missing in action in the far bloodier conflict that followed initially peaceful demonstrations in 2011 to remove the oppressive regime of Bashar Assad in Syria.

Syria's two undemocratic allies, Russia and China, made certain by their veotoes that this time there would be no UN-sanctioned military intervention to stop the slaughter. Concern was also expressed that military intervention could lead to civil war, or even a regional war. But after 18 months and more than 20,000 deaths, the conflict was a civil war, with the government armed by Russia and rebel forces armed and supported by other Middle East countries. By September 2012, the collapse of the Assad regime seemed like a matter of time.

If Libya was a success, the lost wars of Vietnam, Iraq and Afghanistan testify that collective military action can also fail. The economic sanctions that helped bring down South Africa's oppressive apartheid regime testify that peaceful means can sometimes succeed. If the UN's Canadian-initiated *Responsibility to Protect* doctrine can help protect lives and end the rule of killer regimes by sanctions and other peaceful means, far better for the world.

Saving the world from landmines

Years after the shooting and fighting had stopped in many of the war-torn areas across Africa, Asia, the Middle East and elsewhere, civilians were still being killed or maimed at the rate of 26,000 a year in 1999. They were the innocent victims—often children—of war's most deadly detritus, anti-personnel landmines (APLs). Throughout the 1980s and 1990s, APL casualties numbered in the hundreds of thousands, mostly civilians.

The most common APLs are blast mines, planted on or in the ground. Set off by the weight of a foot, the force of the explosion can kill or tear off limbs. Fragmentation mines hurl metal shards at their victims. Bounding Mines jump in the air before exploding and hurling their shards. Most insidious are the small butterfly mines disguised as toys. They are dropped from the air to explode in the hands of whoever picks one up, soldier or child.

In 1992, Jody Williams, U.S. teacher and foreign aid worker, launched a worldwide campaign to ban landmines. Working with just two organizations, Williams founded the International Campaign to Ban Landmines [ICBL]. Five years later, ICBL had grown to 95 non-governmental organizations with 850,000 signatories, and Williams and the ICBL were joint recipients of the Nobel Peace Prize.

By 1995, however, efforts to establish a global API ban at the United Nations had ground to a halt. Canada took the lead in reviving the campaign. With the support of Austria, Belgium and Norway, Foreign Affairs Minister Andre Ouellet arranged a meeting in Geneva for informal talks with the ICBL and the International Committee for the Red Cross. Shortly after, the Red Cross announced that it "is launching its first worldwide campaign in support of a ban on landmines."

In January 1996, Canada became the first country to announce a total ban on the production, export, and use of APLs. It was a symbolic gesture, since Canada had not planted any APLs or other landmines since the Korean War, more than 40 years earlier. But Ouellet still heralded the move. "Canada moves to the forefront of countries seeking a global ban on these weapons," he said.

In May, when government delegates at a UN conference in Geneva agreed to support a treaty to *restrict* the use of APLs, Lloyd Axworthy (who had succeeded Ouellet as foreign affairs minister in January) announced that, in six months, Canada would host a conference in Ottawa to kindle a quest for a *total* ban. When delegates assembled in October, they were surprised when Axworthy announced that there would be yet another conference in another 14 months, with a draft treaty ready for final negotiations and signing.

At the final Ottawa conference that followed, delegates from 122 nations, on December 12, 1997, signed the Ottawa treaty. It is officially known as the *Convention on the Prohibition of the Use, Stockpiling, Production and Transfer of Anti-Personnel Mines and on their Destruction*. Delegates were said to be stunned by how many countries signed on. Jody Williams said, "…it was precisely Canada's willingness to step outside of 'normal' diplomatic process, which was another key element in the success of the ban movement."

Following ratification by the required minimum 40 states, the Ottawa Treaty came into force on March 1, 1999, said to be "the fastest entry-into-force of any multilateral disarmament treaty in history." One hundred fifty eight nations were party to the treaty in 2012. The United States, China, Russia, India, Israel, and North and South Korea are among those not covered by the Treaty.

Some 45 million planted APLs were destroyed by 2011, including a record 388,000 in 2010, according to the ICBL *Landmine Monitor 2011*. The number of annual casualties had been reduced from an estimated 26,000 when the treaty came into force to fewer than 4,200 reported in 2010, although the ICBL says the actual number "was certainly higher" than reported, because of incomplete data collection.

While the ban has reduced the rate of civilian APL casualties by about 80 percent, there are still tens of millions of deadly mines in the stockpiles of the non-treaty nations, and continuing casualties from other unexploded military ordinances. The Ottawa Treaty does not cover mixed mines, anti-tank mines, booby traps, remote-controlled claymore mines, and other unexploded military debris.

Cluster munitions are a continuing menace. They kill and maim civilians long after a conflict has ended. Air dropped or ground launched, they scatter land mines, or hurl explosive bomblets designed to kill, or destroy vehicles, parked airplanes, and other facilities.

A UN Convention on Cluster Munitions came into force in 2010 but has been ratified by only 60 countries, leaving largely unaffected their continued use and buried presence. Four years of negotiations for an alternative treaty intended to gain the adoption of most countries by restricting, rather than completely banning cluster munitions, ended in failure in November 2011. With the opposition of the Red Cross, the ICBL and other humanitarian groups, many countries were unwilling to adopt a treaty that called for less than a total ban and removal of cluster munitions, similar to the Ottawa Treaty for anti-personnel landmines.

From aristocracy to best democracy

We shall have a lasting constitutional liberty, as opposed to democracy. *John A. Macdonald, at the 1864 Quebec Conference that hammered out the framework of Confederation.*

Macdonald was not alone. Many of our founding fathers opposed democracy. The great irony is that their resistance likely helped make Canada arguably the world's best democracy.

Throughout the century from the fall of New France to Confederation, democracy was a weak weed in British North America. The British generals who came to rule as governors general were no democrats. They appointed allies to their advisory executive councils and helped secure elections of the like-minded to the largely powerless assemblies.

Those who governed preached British liberty and practiced aristocracy, comforted by Aristotle's theories of government more than two thousand years earlier. Aristocratic government is undoubtedly splendid—for aristocrats, who enjoy the perks, privileges, power, and wealth.

Canadian democracy ultimately prevailed but it is missing some features of U.S. democracy. For the most part, they are missed like one might miss not having a toothache or the mumps.

But make no mistake. Canadian democracy still has its flaws, it's under pressure as it is everywhere, and a "democratic deficit" is widely assailed.

The autocrat of the Family Compact

At the apex of aristocratic rule was the notorious Family Compact, which oppressed, suppressed and exploited Upper Canada during most of the first four decades of the nineteenth century.

The Family Company's *éminence grise* was The Right Reverend John Strachan, first Bishop of Toronto, founder of the University of Toronto, a member of both the executive council and the assembly, president of the Board of Education, chairman of the Clergy Corporation, and the most powerful politician of his day.

Strachan came to Canada a 21-year-old schoolteacher of modest means who, he wrote, "dreamed of riches and honour." He found both.

He seldom missed a rant against democracy. He dismissed responsible government as "an insane paradox" where "all is corruption."[1] He complained that the elected Assembly was "composed of ignorant clowns, for the spirit of leveling seems to pervade the province." He warned against good Canadian boys attending American universities where they would "commonly learn little beyond anarchy in Politics & infidelity in religion."[2]

When social reformer Robert Gourlay undertook "A well authenticated statistical account of social and economic conditions" in Upper Canada, based on a survey of 31 questions (How many farm animals do you own? How many schools and churches in your district? How can conditions be improved?)[3] Strachan branded him a "dangerous radical." He wrote a friend: "A character like Mr. Gourlay in a quiet colony like this where there is little or no spirit of inquiry and very little knowledge can do much harm by exciting uneasiness and unreasonable hopes."[4]

When the Bishop of Quebec proposed to petition settlers on a church matter, Strachan protested, in part because of "its democratic aspects… I am quite satisfied that in this province the plan of petitioning the people will be followed by many evils."[5] He said British settlers would be welcome in Upper Canada, except "levelers and democrats." He protested a British Parliamentary report, which, he said, would "Strengthen the Levellers and Democrats."[6]

Newspapers controlled by the government and its supporters echoed the anti-democracy rants.

The *Upper Canada Gazette,*[7] boldly forecast the failure of republican government in the United States:

"Viewing all republics, ancient as well as modern, as so many imperfect systems of government, differing only in their respective degrees of imperfection, we consider the growth and extension of the Federal Government of the United States, as a subject of deepest interest—as an experiment on a large scale of a system which, it appears to us is contrary to the universal order of nature, from the Divinity, downwards, to the communities of the meanest insects; and so satisfied are we of the impossibility of any long duration of the present order of things in the United States—that we have no doubt there are many now living who will see an entire disruption of the North American Federal Government."

The *Brockville Gazette*[8] warned that democracy rests "…upon the whim and caprice of a vain and arrogant people [and] has a tendency to blunt, and ultimately do away with the finer feelings of humanity." It claimed that in the United States "the ideas and sentiments peculiar to what are emphatically styled gentlemen in England, are almost unknown… and in lieu of them little is to be found except an all absorbing thirst of gain." Americans were said to be "cajoled by the rich, who do in fact despise the poor more than any aristocracy." Believing that they had no superiors, Americans were said to "feel no inclination to respect any station more exalted than that to which a notorious slave dealer is eligible."

There were, of course, democratic voices, none louder than William Lyon Mackenzie, who praised American democracy in his *Colonial Advocate.* Or at least he did until, as a fugitive from his failed 1837 rebellion, he lived in the United States, where he witnessed, he reported, democracy riddled with corruption.

Things we gladly miss

Embers from these and other anti-democratic and oppressive episodes of a long bygone era have cast a lasting mark on Canadian democracy, in which we miss some of the more democratic features of our southern neighbour. A few of the thing we miss are:

Election excess. Election of sheriffs, prosecuting attorneys and judges, and the elevation of jurists to the Supreme Court based on political ideology or partisanship.

Dollar democracy. Virtually unrestrained election spending of billions of dollars by Big Business, Big Unions and Big Billionaires helps secure the best politicians that money can buy.

Guns. Laws that permit carrying concealed guns into offices, schools and churches contribute to the highest rate of homicides among the world's 20 most prosperous nations.

Healthcare. The United States is the only industrialized nation that fails to provide universal public health care. Americans spend, per person, more on health care than any other nation with results that are generally worse than in most affluent countries.

Ontario Archives

Bishop John Strachan, eminence grise of the Family Compact in Upper Canada, led the aristocratic attack on democracy and "levellers," asserting that "petitioning the people will be followed by many evils."

U.S. infant mortality rate, for example, is 20 percent greater than in Canada, almost double Sweden's rate. In terms of life expectancy, the United States ranks last (average 78 years at birth) on a list of 50 countries; Canada ranks 11th, at 81 years.

Market ideology. Reliance on the self-correcting discipline of free markets in lieu of regulation of banks and brokers resulted in the 2008 collapse of financial institutions and the worst economic recession in six decades. Millions of Americans lost their jobs, their savings, their homes, and their hopes.

Alan Greenspan, a disciple of Ayn Rand and an icon of market self-regulation under whose 18-year rule as chairman of the U.S. Federal Reserve the market ideology held sway, told a U.S. Congressional committee, after the collapse, that he had been wrong. Asked if he had been "pushed" by ideology "to make decisions that you wish you had not made," Greenspan responded: "Yes, I've found a flaw... I've been very distressed by that fact... I was shocked, because I have been going on for 40 years or more with very considerable evidence that it [free market self-regulation] was working exceptionally well."[9]

The lesson of 2008 is that business competition cannot function without rules and regulators, any more than hockey, basketball, or football can be played without rules and referees. Without regulation, business implodes, as it did so spectacularly with the fall of financial giants that were "too big to fail."

The job of regulation is not to supplant market competition, but to ensure that it works. Governments must also prohibit, avert or mitigate unintended adverse side effects of business, or any other human activity. A prime example is the cause or contribution to global warming from producing and burning fossils fuels.

Political gridlock. When a Congressional majority opposes a U.S. administration, nothing much is what often happens. That gridlock killed hopes for universal health care. It stalled measures by Barack Obama to revive the U.S. economy and relieve the distress of the unemployed.

In Europe, we have seen the economic effects of dysfunctional democracy in countries such as Greece and Italy, which brought ruin and suffering to these countries, pushed the European Union to the brink of break-up, and threatened the world with renewed economic recession.

World's best democracy?

There are many attributes to support an argument that Canada has the world's best democracy. We can briefly summarize at least a few of these attributes.

•Where in the world are personal liberty and fundamental rights in better balance with collective welfare—the common good?

•Governance. Almost alone among industrialized nations, Canada largely escaped the ravages of the 2008 economic recession, thanks in large measure to one aspect of good governance. Strong earnings from natural resources, especially oil and natural gas, helped. But sound regulation of banks and other financial institutions was key to averting the type of collapse that toppled the United States and Europe into deep and lingering recession.

•Peacefulness. Canada is in the top five percent of the world's most peaceful country, as ranked in 2011 by the Global Peace Index.

•Quality of life. Canada ranks second for quality of life, among 34 nations assessed by the OECD in 2011.

•Social harmony. There are few nations with greater social harmony and less racial and ethnic tensions than Canada. That's perhaps largely because Canada has greater cultural, racial and ethnic diversity than any other country.

Such features provide at least a case for argument. But here, as elsewhere around the globe, democracy faces constant challenge. Critics argue that Canada already suffers a democratic deficit, and that it is under further assault by our national government.

(Endnotes)
1 Strachan, John. "Documents and Opinions." J.L.H. Henderson, editor.)Toronto: McClelland and Stewart, 1969).
2 Craig, G.M. "John Strachan." Dictionary of Canadian Biography, online.
3 Milani, Lois Darroch. "Robert Gourlay, Gad Fly. (Toronto: Ampersand Press, 1971).
4 Strachan. "Memoir." A.N. Bethune, editor. (Toronto: Henry Rowser, 1870).
5 Strachan. "Documents and Opinions."
6 Craig, Dictionary of Canadian Biography.
7 *Upper Canada Gazette,* York (Toronto), July 7, 1825.
8 *Brockville Gazette,* December 26, 1818.
9 *New York Times,* October 23, 2008.

Abuse of power

Democracy might be the best known guarantor of human rights and economic wellbeing, but it has been blemished by bouts of abuse and corruption everywhere, at every time. In Canada, both Liberal and Conservative governments, with their exclusive hold on national office since Confederation, have had their share of scandals, from the Conservative Government of John A. Macdonald (see Headline History in Chapter Six) to the Conservative government of Stephen Harper. The most recent Liberal case was the AdScam scandal that diverted to the Liberal Party perhaps as much as $3 million of government funds intended to promote federalism in Quebec.

"A series of highly publicized confrontations... have lead many observers to conclude that the Harper government is at war with its public service."

Charges leveled against the Harper government have been limited to abuse of power, rather than financial gain for party, politicians, or supporters. The list of abuses, alleged and established, is daunting: waging war on the civil service; covering up allegations of complicity in the torture (and possibly extrajudicial killings and disappearances) of Afghan war prisoners; contempt of Parliament; silencing critics by coercion, intimidation, firings and character assassination; illegally disclosing private, personal information; illegally withholding public information; promoting export sales of cacogenic Canadian asbestos, in the face of universal condemnation; policies that curb news media reporting of government activity; sponsoring crime legislation for political advantage in the knowledge of evidence that such policies do not work.

We'll look briefly at some of these issues in this and following items.

CIVIL SERVICE WAR

"A series of highly publicized confrontations between the Harper Conservatives and senior government officials, as well as direct intervention in the operation of arms' length agencies, elimination of advisory

bodies and rejection of expert advice have led many observers to conclude that the Harper government is at war with its public service." Brooke Jeffrey, political science professor.[1]

The Harper administration is not the first national Conservative (or Progressive Conservative) government to display "suspicion, mistrust and a deep-seated conviction that the public service is biased in favour of the Liberal Party," as noted by Jeffrey. But the degree of conflict between the Harper administration and the public service seems unprecedented.

Undoubtedly the Harper administration is frustrated by a conviction that the bureaucracy too often frustrates its philosophy, policy and programs. Much of the bureaucracy, in turn, is convinced the government employs intimidation, coercion, character assassination, subversion of good governance and democratic practice, and even illegal means, in pursuit of its objectives.

More than half the federal civil servants surveyed in a Queen's University study said they had been subjected to "undue political interference" by the political staff of the prime minister, cabinet ministers and other senior politicians. Most felt that the political staffers were not capable of handling their responsibilities, and lacked adequate training for their jobs.[2]

Civil servants claim the government has failed to live up to its promise to protect those who report wrongdoing in the government. That promise was a key plank in the 2006 Conservative election platform. "We have worked to protect whistleblowers by passing ironclad protections for those whistleblowers in the Federal Accountability Act," Pierre Poilievre, Harper's parliamentary secretary, told the Commons in 2007.

But that's not what's happening, according to a report released in February 2012 by the Public Sector Integrity Commissioner. Civil servants who participated in 10 focus groups across the country claimed that whistleblowers face reprisals, while wrongdoing is often unreported.

"Most employees see reprisals for disclosing wrongdoing as a real possibility, primarily because of the subtle form they can take," the report states. "What this means concretely in the minds of many participants was that the disclosure of wrongdoing would end up being the one punished, not the perpetrator."

Lack of advancement, exclusion from meetings, poor performance evaluations, and being ostracized were perceived as forms of reprisal.

Lack of anonymity and protection for whistleblowers as well as little awareness of how to report wrongdoing, were seen as problems.

"Show me the stories" of whistleblowers "that have happy endings," said one civil servant, quoted in the report. "Show me the disclosure who got a promotion and the wrongdoer who lost his job."

The career of Canada's first protector of whistleblowers ended with suggestions of a coverup. Christine Ouimet was officially Canada's first Public Sector Integrity Commissioner, appointed in 2007. During her 38 months in office, she found no wrongdoing in the federal public service, despite receiving 228 complaints. When Auditor General Sheila Fraser investigated, Ouimet resigned, with a $530,000 severance package that prohibits her from talking about what went on. Two months later, Fraser's report concluded that allegations of improper performance by Ouimet "are founded." Complaints of wrongdoing and reprisals against complainers were said to have been either dismissed, not investigated, or the investigations not completed.

A further investigation by auditing firm Deloitte and Touche for the Integrity Commission found no less than 114 problems in handling files. David Hutton, executive director of advocacy group Federal Accountability Initiative Reform (FAIR), complained that the investigation was too restrictive, because auditors lacked power to interview either Ouimet's employees or whistleblowers. "There are mishandled cases" that are four to six years old, Hutton told the *Ottawa Citizen May* 18, 2011. "Those whistleblowers have been living with this, some suffering reprisals and losing their jobs."

THOSE WHO DISASGREED

The number of senior civil servants who have disagreed with the government and are no longer employed, can be seen as another indicator of the conflict between government and the civil service. The list of some of the more prominent departed was summarized in the Toronto *National Post,* August 18, 2010:

"Linda Keen, president of the Canadian Nuclear Safety Commission, which shut down the nuclear reactor in Chalk River, Ont. over safety concerns. The government,

worried about the impact on medical isotopes, said it had lost confidence in her and terminated her appointment…

"Pat Stogran, a vocal veterans' ombudsman who complained of bureaucratic obstruction" did not have his term renewed.

"Steven Sullivan, the victims of crime ombudsman, whose term was not renewed" after criticizing the government's tough-on-crime agenda.

"Sheridan Scott, the Competition Bureau head, who ran afoul of the environment minister and quit… after being told her appointment would not be renewed.

"Paul Kennedy, the head of the RCMP Public Complaints Commission, who lobbied for more power for his commission, and whose term was not renewed.

"Peter Tinsley, the chair of the Military Complaints Commission, whose appointment was not renewed in December 2009, just as his commission was investigating the controversial issue of Afghan detainee transfers.

"Adrian Measner, president of the Canadian Wheat Board, whose appointment was terminated in December 2006, after disagreeing with the government on the board's monopoly over the sale of barley and wheat.

"Bernard Shapiro, the ethics commissioner who clashed repeatedly with Harper and quit suddenly in March 2007.

"Munir Sheikh, the chief statistician of Statistic Canada, who quit… after the government killed the long-form census and then defended the move by publicly (and inaccurately) suggesting it had the support of Sheikh's agency."

MUZZLED MEDIA

Add news media to the chorus complaining about politically-slanted government information control, with a media muzzle that extends to illegal denial of public documents.

"Under Prime Minister Stephen Harper, the flow of information out of Ottawa has slowed to a trickle," the presidents of nine national and provincial legislative press galleries advised members of the Canadian Association of Journalists in an open letter, June 2010. "Cabinet ministers and civil servants are muzzled. Access to information requests are stalled and stymied by political interference. Genuine transparency is replaced by slick propaganda and spin designed to manipulate public opinion."

Critical journalists are said to be black-balled. Photographers and videographers are barred from public events featuring Conservative politicians. In their place, photos and footage shot by the prime minister's press staff are blitzed to newsrooms across Canada, so that "Canadians only get a sanitized and staged version of history." Information sought from government "scientists, doctors, regulators, auditors and policy experts" elicit email responses from "an armada of press officers who know very little or nothing about a reporter's topic and who answer tough questions" with vetted talking points.[3]

Kathryn O'Hara, president of the 500-member Canadian Science Writers' Association, followed up the CJA letter with an open letter to Harper, urging him to "Take off the muzzle" from government scientists. Scientists, wrote O'Hara, must be allowed to speak for themselves "about state of ice in the Arctic, dangers in the food supply, nanotechnology, salmon viruses, radiation monitoring, or how much the climate will change."[4]

O'Hara cited the experience of Fisheries and Oceans scientist Kristia Miller. Miller was denied permission to respond to media inquiries about her groundbreaking studies of West Coast salmon diseases. She was also told not to attend workshops at which scientists were to discuss the issue, because the Department didn't want the media to hear what she might say.

Globe and Mail reporter Mark Hume likened the government's muzzle on scientists to "a paranoid dictatorship."

WITHHOLDING INFORMATION

Complaints about delays, denials and blacked-out (redacted) responses to information requested under the *Access to Information Act* were given weight by Information Commissioner Suzanne Legault, in a March 2011 special report to Parliament.

On July 28, 2009, a reporter with Canadian Press submitted, under the *Act,* a request for a 133-page report on the management of the government's real estate portfolio. Thirty days later, the last date for legal compliance with a request, the document was in the mailroom of the Department of Public Works and Government Services, ready for delivery. It was retrieved from the mailroom and withheld in response to instructions emailed from Sebastein Togneri, a political staffer in the office of Public Works Minister Christian Paradis. Fifty-two days later, 15 pages of the document were released to Canadian Press.

"Ministerial staff members have no authority to make any decisions under the Act or give any directions to institution officials," Legault ruled in her report to Parliament about the incident. "There are serious consequences for the rights of requesters when political staff members overstep their mandate and compromise a process that was designed to be objective and non-partisan."

Legault also expressed concern about officials who fail to say "no" to unauthorized requests from political staffers, and about provisions of the *Act* that make it impossible for her to refer "interference involving political staff members to law enforcement agencies."

EXPORTING CANCER

Promoting exports of Canadian asbestos promotes sales of a toxic substance more deadly than cigarettes. Its use in Canada is virtually prohibited, millions of dollars have been spent to remove asbestos installation in buildings, its use is banned in scores of countries, including the Europe Union and the United States. Yet the Canadian and Quebec governments continued to support sales of Canadian asbestos to those impoverished countries that have not yet banned its use. Canada's action is opposed by the World Health Organization; the International Labour Organization; 137 of the 143 member nations of the Rotterdam Convention on hazardous substances; 26 Canadian health and environmental organization; the federal government's own Department of Health,[5] and more than 100 scientists from 28 countries, who wrote an open letter to Quebec Premier Jean Charest[6]. "In Quebec itself, exposure to asbestos is the single biggest cause of worker deaths," the scientists wrote. "Your government is spending millions of dollars to remove asbestos while at the same time exporting it to developing countries and telling them it is safe."

Hope of resusitating Canada's 130-year old asbestos mining industry—shut in for more than a year—died September 4, 2012, with the new government of Premier Pauline Marois Quebec committed to cancelling a $58 million loan to reopen the Jeffrey mine in the town of Asbestos.

"The Harper government has this weird contempt for solid evidence," Jeffrey Simpson wrote in the *Globe and Mail*. "Some day, many years and many failures from now, it will fall to some other government to undo these matters."

Endnotes
1 Brooke Jeffrey, Concordia University, Department of Political Science, Canadian Political Science Association, May 17, 2011.
2 Birch, Julie and Thomas Axworthy, Closing the Implementation Gap: Improving capacity, accountability, performance and human resource quality in the Canadian and Ontario public service." Centre for the Study of Democracy, Queen's University, 2010.
3 Buzzetti, Hélèn et al, "An Open Letter to Canadian Journalists, Canadian Journalist Association, http://www.caj.ca/?p=692by, accessed February 5, 2012.
4 Hume, Mark. "Writers want Ottawa to let scientists "speak for themselves, "Globe and Mail, January 22, 2012.
5 CBC, June 13, 2011. CBC reported that the federal government rejected the department's advice that Canada join more than 100 other nations in approving listing asbestos as a hazardous substance under the Rotterdam convention.
6 Journal of Occupational and Environmental Health, April 10, 2010.

The F-35 fighter jet faced an uncertain future in 2012, with "years of testing still to go."

Two trillion dollar jet fighter debacle

Trillions of long-term dollars, including billions of Canadian taxpayer money, were at issue in 2012 in a multinational effort to develop the world's most costly piece of military equipment, while the effort teetered on the edge of collapse. In Canada, the planned fighter jets produced a scandal of bureaucratic bungling and political coverup, misinformation, and contempt of Parliamentary democracy.

The F-35 Lightning II Joint Strike Fighter jet aircraft is a manned, single-engine, multipurpose, fifth generation plane, under development by 11 countries since 1996. They planned to acquire 3,100 of the jet fighters; more than 2,400 by the United States, 65 by Canada and the rest by Britain, Australia, Italy, Turkey, Norway, Denmark, the Netherlands, Japan and Israel.

"Manned fighter jets are essential to our ability to maintain and control sovereignty over our air space," Chief of Staff Lieutenant-General André Deschamps assured the House of Commons Defence Committee in 2010. Deschamps claimed that "Only a fifth generation fighter" can meet Canada's requirements, and Lightning II is the only fifth generation aircraft available to Canada.[1]

Two years later, after spending 16 years and $400 million helping develop the F-35 Lightning II and bolstering its aerospace industry to join in building the planes, Canada seemed likely to cancel its planned purchase. Cost estimates had risen and anticipated delivery dates were delayed and uncertain.

The government needed to replace what was left of the 138 CF-18 Hornet jet fighters it purchased in 1980 for $4 billion. Their useful lifespan was originally expected to expire in 2003. Extensive modernization and retrofitting had extended this for a few of the remaining Hornets to between 2017 and 2020. Upgrading and retrofitting CF-18 Hornets cost an estimated $2.6 billion. Only 77 of the upgraded Hornets were still in service in 2012. There was no certainty what the cost of the F-35s would be, whether they would be available before the extended life of those 77 Hornets expired, how much longer more fixing up could keep them flying, and at what cost. If the F-35 is abandoned and a competition is held to pick an alternative fighter jet, "It will cost taxpayers $1 billion and will create an operational gap for the air force," according to Defence Minister Peter MacKay.[2]

Long tribulations
of a fighter jet

There were three phases to the Joint Strike Fighter (JSF) program that would span decades to develop and produce all the 3,100 planned jets: concept design, system development and demonstration, and continued development and production.

The program started in late 1996 when the U.S. Defence Department awarded $750 million contracts each to the Boeing Company and Lockheed Martin Corporation to produce a pair of concept aircraft. Canada, under the Liberal government of Jean Chretien, signed on to this phase the next year, with a US$10.6 million commitment spelled out in a memorandum of understanding.

Lockheed's concept aircraft won the competition, and in November 2002, Canada joined in the system and development phase, committing an additional US$150 million to the program.

The driving force behind this commitment was not the need to replace the CF-18 Hornets, nor about Canada's defence requirements, according to Alan Williams, who signed this second memorandum of understanding as the defence department's assistant deputy minister in charge of procuring military equipment. The purpose "had nothing to do with buying these jets," Williams told the Commons Standing Committee on National Defence, speaking after he had retired from the department. The entire purpose, he said, was to provide "an opportunity for Canada's aerospace industry" to compete for F-35 contract work. "If Canada did not participate, its industry would not even be provided the opportunity to compete… This possibility was one we could not contemplate, and so Canada entered the program."[3]

And compete it did, at least in this phase. The industry won 144 contracts for US$490 million in work from 2002 to 20012. There was also a prospect of an estimated US$4.8 billion to US$6.8 billion by the time the last of the fighter jets were expected to be in the air.[4]

On December 13, 2006, Canada committed up to another US$510 million for on going development, testing, and support of the F-35 over a 45-year period, in the third phase of the program. Including the two earlier phases, the total could grow to as much as US$710 million, Auditor General Michael Ferguson later reported.[5] That didn't include billions of dollars in purchase and operating costs if Canada later decided to buy the then-planned 80-jets. "We are convinced the aircraft is going to be a technological marvel… superior probably to everything else that's out there," Michael Slack, the Defence Department's director of the JSF program, told *Canadian Press.* While the Liberals committed to the first two phases, it was Stephen Harper's Conservative who, less than a year after coming to power, signed up for the costly third phase.

Two days after Canada signed on for the third and final phase of the JSF development program, the first JSF F-35 Lighting II fighter jet test aircraft took flight. Sixty-three test planes were produce over five years in a process the military dubbed "concurrency." The process involved concurrent computer design, manufacturing the aircraft, and test flights, followed by more design, repairs and retrofits to correct deficiencies revealed during the tests. Concurrent work turned out to be a major problem. The process was foolish, the head of the U.S. Air Force later admitted. "There was a view that we… could design an airplane that would be near perfect the first time it flew," General Norton Schwartz, U.S. Air Force Chief of Staff, told a conference of aerospace industry investors. "I think we actually believed that. And I think we've demonstrated in a compelling way that that's foolishness."[6]

The government's decision to purchase the F-35 appears to have been made in 2008, although it was not publicly announced for another two years. A 21-page *Canada First Defence Strategy,* released with fanfare at a news conference held by Prime Minister Harper and Peter MacKay May 21, states:

"Starting in 2017, 65 next generation fighter jets [are] to replace the existing fleet of CF-18s." That could refer only to the F-35 Lightning II jets.

The political storm breaks

Peter MacKay's announcement July 16, 2010 confirming that the government had decided to purchase 65 of the fighter jets (15 fewer than originally planned) triggered a storm of controversy that grew only louder during the next two years. The announced purchase price was $9 billion. No mention was made of development, operating, and maintenance costs. Delivery of the first planes was expected in 2016.

Liberal Leader Michael Ignatieff called for immediate hearings by the Commons Defence Committee, blasted a "secretive, unaccountable decision," and promised that a Liberal government would put the sole-source contract on hold.

The government and the military were staunch in their defence of the planned purchase and the critics were strident in their opposition, during the months that followed.

"This is the right plane. This is the right number. This is the right aircraft for our Canadian forces and for Canada," MacKay told the Defence Committee. "If we don't make this purchase there is a real danger we'll be unable to defend our airspace, unable to exercise our sovereignty or unable to share our responsibility to both NORAD and NATO."

"Head and shoulders above" any alternative aircraft to "address the security needs of Canada," former chief of air staff Lieutenant General Angus Watt, told *Maclean's.*

The critics were not appeased. Lack of

competitive bidding was one bone of contention. Alan Williams, the retired Defence Department procurement chief who talked about the second phase of the JSF program in remarks to the Defence Committee, talked also about the decision to buy the aircrafts. He said government's stated reasons for flouting policy requirements for competitive bids were "all flawed," and "insult our intelligence." Only by "rigorous examination" of competitive proposals can the government be certain "which aircraft best meets Canadian requirements." Sole-sourcing, he noted, had dramatically increased to more than 42 percent of Defence Department's purchase contracts. "Sole-source deals leave the procurement process more vulnerable to fraud, bribery, and behind-the scenes deal making," risking billions of dollars in potential losses.[7]

William's concerns about the Defence Department's procurement process were amplified 19 days later in the final report of retiring Auditor General Sheila Fraser. In auditing the purchase of new military helicopters, Fraser found "troubling" systemic problems, rigged competitions, and cost overruns in procurement programs. The contract award process for the helicopters failed to comply with regulations and policies, and "was not fair, open, and transparent," Fraser wrote.

Other critics claimed the F-35's short range and single engine were unsuited for patrolling an air space as big as Canada's. The CF-18 Hornets were chosen, in large part, because twin engines were considered essential for long-range patrols of Canada's vast Arctic and coastal spaces.

Retired Major General Leonard Johnson questioned the need for any fighter jets. "It's hard to see any useful military role for the F-35 Joint Strike Fighters," with the passing of the age of major interstate war, Johnson wrote in the *Ottawa Citizen*.[8] Yet six months later, Canada's Hornets flew 10 percent of the NATO missions that struck Libya's military to enforce a UN-sanctioned no-fly zone, leading to the overthrow of dictator Moammar Gadhafi. The Hornets were pressed near their limits, raising concern about the possible effect on the ancient machines.[9]

If the government had intended to sow confusion about its commitment to the F-35 and the cost, it could hardly have done a better job. "Mr. Speaker, let us look at the actual contract," MacKay said in Commons Debate.[10] "What the Canadian government has committed to is a $9 billion contract for the acquisition of 65 fifth generation aircraft." In fact, there was no purchase contract, and no commitment: there was simply an announcement that this is what the government had decided to do.

As for cost, MacKay used only one figure in his public statements, $9 billion, the stated acquisition cost. "I have no idea where these other figures are coming from," he told the Conference of Defence Associations. "They're simply made up—or they're guessing.[11] Perhaps MacKay should have talked to Laurie Hawn, his Parliamentary assistant, who was more forthcoming in Parliamentary debate. "In fact, the total cost we are talking about for 20 years, plus the acquisition of the airplane, is $16 billion," Hawn told MPs.[12] In actual fact, Hawn must have—or certainly should have—known that the government's undisclosed estimate of the total 20-year cost was $9 billion more than he told Parliament.

Cost estimates became the focus of Parliamentary debate in 2011, not only the cost of the F-35s but also the cost of the government's tough-on-crime bills, whose mandatory sentences are expected to send more people to jail for longer periods. The opposition parties demanded to see the documents supporting the cost figures. The government refused.

Demands to see the F-35 cost documents intensified on March 10 when Parliamentary Budget Officer Kevin Page released a report that estimated the lifetime costs of the jets at $29 billion, almost double what the government had been saying. In response to the Page report, the government released an even lower cost estimate, $14.7 billion. But it still refused to release either the F-35 or crime bill documents. "There is no doubt the order to produce documents is not being complied with, and this goes to the heart of the House's undoubted role in holding the government to account," House Speaker Peter Milligan ruled. Two weeks after the Page report was released, the government fell on a contempt of Parliament motion based on its refusal to release the documents. It is the only government in the Commonwealth of Nations to fall on contempt of parliamentary democracy. National elections were called the day the government fell, March 25.

Re-elected with its first majority in the House, the government was all gung-ho for the F-35. "We will purchase the F-35," Associate Defence Minister Julian Fantino vowed at a November news conference in Fort Worth, Texas, where the fleet of F-35 test planes are being built. "We're on record. We're part of the crusade. We are not backing down."[13]

That fierce stance wilted under a barrage of continuing F-35 problems throughout 2012.

January 13: "The program has demonstrated very little missions system capability," says a U.S. Defence Department report. The 63 test planes "will require significant numbers of structural modifications and upgrades to attain the planned service life."[14]

January 26: U.S. Defence Department to defer 179 of the 429 F-35's it had planned to order in the next five years, to help cut $259 billion from total military spending during that period, *Reuters* reports.

February 11. Fantino hosts a meeting of countries in the F-35 program at the Canadian Embassy in Washington to discuss adverse cost implications of the U.S. slowdown.

March 13: Four months after vowing Canada would not back down Fatino tells the Commons Defence Committee, "The… decision has not been made as to whether or not we are actually going to purchase, buy, acquire the F-35… we have not as yet discounted the possibility, of course, [of] backing out of the program. None of the partners have."

March 20: The plan to produce affordable F-35s in large numbers "could be in question," the U.S. Government Accountability Office warns in a report to Congress. "Full production rate has been delayed five years, and initial operational capabilities are now unsettled," Michael Sullivan, GAO's director of acquisitions, tells a Congressional committee. Projected funding needs of more than $13 billion a year for the next 23 years were said to be "unprecedented," with "risks of additional cost overruns and retrofit cost," from flight testing that "has years to go." Sullivan blamed "most of the instability in the program" on "highly concurrent development, testing and production."[15]

April 2: Pentagon documents estimate the full, lifetime costs of the government's planned 2,457 F-35s at $1.5 trillion, up from $1.38 trillion a year earlier, *Reuters* reports.[16] The cost is $615 million per jet fighter. Norway has estimated the lifetime costs of its planned 55 F-35 jets at $769 million each.[17]

The U.S. and Norwegian estimates suggest a lifetime costs for Canada's 65 jets at $39-50 billion, about $10-20 billion more than even Kevin Pages' estimate.

The full lifetime cost of all the 3,100 fighter jets that had been planned seemed likely to exceed $2 trillion. But the number on order is declining, as most—perhaps all—countries reduce or cancel their planned purchases. Japan has joined Canada in considering whether to buy any; the Dutch have cancelled their planned 65; Britain has reduced its planned purchases by 90; Australia has committed for only two of its planned 100; Italy has committed for only 19 of its planned 75 planes; others are likely to follow suit. In mid-September, the United States said that there would be no further increases to its F-35 budget; continued cost overruns would mean further deferral of purchases, reduced capabilities, or fewer planes. As the order book shrinks, the price of each jet expands.

Meanwhile, Canada's need to replace its ancient CF-18 Hornets grows increasingly urgent. The 77 still in service are more than three-quarters of the way through their already extended life expectancy. On September 28, the Australian National Audit Office warned that the use of that country's 71 Hornets needs to be scaled back to avert structural fatigue concerns. Annual maintenance cost for the Australian fleet was forecast to almost double, from $AUS118 million in 2001, to $214 million by 2018. The outlook for Canada's similar vintage Hornets can hardly be any better.

> **"This is about whether...billions of public dollars can be appropriated without the informed consent of the public. It is about whether we live in a functioning Parliamentary democracy, or want to."**

"There is no moving on from a lie this big"

A full year after the government ignored the Speaker of the House and defied Parliamentary democracy, Auditor General Michael Ferguson, in his April 4, 2012 report to Parliament, disclosed the $25 billion cost estimate that the government had kept under wraps.

The Defence Department was accused of lack of due diligence in the procurement process, with general bungling, improper procedures, withholding documents, and providing false information, among other things. Public Works was castigated for blindly accepting the Defence Department strategy, which "compromised an important control in the procurement process."

The big issue in the uproar, however, was misleading Parliament and the public about the cost. The opposition parties laid the blame at the top, on the shoulders of Prime Minister Harper. "He cannot now pretend that he was just the piano player in the brothel who didn't have a clue as to what was really going on upstairs," said Liberal Leader Bob Rae.

Among the political pundits, none were more outraged than conservative journalists, particularly two columnists who write for the *National Post* and the Postmedia chain of newspapers. "So that's it then: They knew and they lied," wrote Michael Den Tandt. "There is no moving on from a lie this big."

"This is about whether departments are answerable to their ministers, and whether ministers are answerable to Parliament—or whether billions of public dollars can be appropriated without the informed consent of either Parliament or the public," Andrew Coyne wrote. "It is about whether we live in a functioning Parliamentary democracy, or want to."

(Endnotes)

1 House of Commons Standing Committee on National Defence (Defence Committee), September 15, 2010.

2 Speech, Conference of Defence Associations, February 25, 2011.

3 Alan S. Williams, Defence Committee, October 7, 2010.

4 Williams. *Reinventing Canadian Defence Procurement: A View From the Inside.* Kingston, Breakout Education Network, Queen's University, 2006.

5 Michael Ferguson, *Report of the Auditor General of Canada to the House of Commons,* April 4, 2012.

6 Marcus Weisgerber, "DoD Anticipates Better Price on Next F-35 Batch," *Defense News,* March 8, 2012.

7 Defence Committee, September 15, 2010.

8 *Ottawa Citizen,* September 23, 2010.

9 Murray Brewster, *Wear tear on CF-18 fleet worried Air Force planners.* Canadian Press, September 10, 2012.

10 December 13, 2010.

11 Speech, February 25, 2011.

12 March 10, 2011.

13 News media reports, news conference, Fort Worth, Texas, November 8, 2011.

14 Tony Capaccio, "F-35 Showed Mixed Results in Tests," *Bloomberg*, January 13, 2012.

15 Michael J. Sullivan, Director, Acquisitions and Sourcing Management, U.S. Government Accountability Office. Prepared statement on testimony presented to the Subcommittee on Tactical Air and Land Forces, Committee on Armed Services, House of Representative, Washington, March 30, 2012.

16 Andrea Shalal-Esa, "Government sees lifetime cost of F-35 fighter at $1.51 trillion." *Reuters,* April 2, 2012.

17 Norwegian Rear Admiral Arne Roksund, House of Commons National Defence Committee, Ottawa, November 24, 2011.

Demagoguery and failed crime laws

"Every time we proposed amendments to the Criminal Code, sociologists, criminologists, defence lawyers, and Liberals attacked us for proposing measures that the evidence apparently showed did not work. That was a good thing for us politically, in that sociologists, criminologists, and defence lawyers were and are all held in lower repute than Conservatives politically by the voting public. Politically it helped us tremendously to be attacked by this coalition of university types." *Ian Brodie, political science professor and Stephen Harper's chief of staff 2006-2008, at a McGill University symposium, March 2009.*

The proper term for Brodie's depiction of Conservative government strategy is demagoguery: mining the depth of public attitudes and emotions for political support.

We do not know how many billions of dollars it will cost to build the extra jails and lodge more prisoners for longer periods, as mandated by *The Safe Streets and Community Act,* passed by Parliament in December 2011. The Act amends more than half a dozen crime laws. We do not know the cost because the Harper government refused to disclose its estimates, in defiance of Parliamentary democracy, as it did with its estimated cost to purchase F-35 fighter jets.

We do know that whatever the costs, Bill C-10, legislating *Safe Streets and Community Act,* was passed at a time when Canada's streets and communities were safer than they had been in decades, possibly half a century. In 2010, "Canada's Violent Crime Severity Index fell six percent, the fourth consecutive annual decline and the largest drop seen in more than a decade," Statistics Canada reported five months before Bill C-10 was passed. "With 554 homicides in 2010, the homicide rate dropped 10 percent to its lowest point since the mid 1960s," says Statistics Canada's *Police-reported crime statistics in Canada, 2010.* "The rate of attempted murders also fell (by 14 percent) and reached its lowest point since 1977."

The decades-long decline in almost all crime seems to affirm the success of decades of criminal justice focused on prevention and rehabilitation, as opposed to wholesale imprisonment.

We do not know whether the *Act* will make streets and communities safer, as the government claims, or more dangerous, as critics claim. We do know that similar U.S. tough-on-crime laws have failed, and are now being abandoned in favour of more prevention and less imprisonment, in such states as Texas and California. From 1975 to 2005, U.S. incarceration increased 700 percent. With 2.3 million of its citizens locked up, the United States, with five percent of the world population, housed 25 percent of the world's prisoners. U.S. violent crime has also been declining, but remains much higher than in Canada. There were 14,748 reported murders U.S. in 2010, a rate of 4.8 murders for every 100,000 Americans, precisely three times the rate of 1.6 murders for every 100,000 Canadians.

At hearings before the Parliamentary Committee on Justice and Human Rights in the final months of 2011, opponents of Bill C-10 included six provincial and territorial governments, and organizations and individuals ranging from the Canadian Bar Association to David Daubney, former chair of the Parliamentary Justice committee and a senior policy advisor in the Department of Justice for more than 20 years. Supporters included four provincial governments (Alberta, Saskatchewan, Manitoba, and British Columbia), police forces, federal government officials, and families of victims of criminal violence.

Not all violence victims supported the legislation. Wilma Derksen, a Winnipeg mother of a 13-year-old daughter who was abducted and murdered, said she spoke for a group of victims who opposed the legislation. "The answer to crime is to put our energy and creative thinking into giving our young people better education and a better life," Derksen told the committee. "I wonder if we can afford to focus so many of our scarce resources on locking up the past so that there are only crumbs left for the living who are struggling to find hope for the future."

The dollar costs of sending more people to serve longer terms in jail, and a diminished focus on crime prevention and rehabilitation, are the two biggest concerns of most critics of the new tough-on-crime laws. Yet warnings have also been sounded about an imminent breakdown of over-burdened courtroom work, trouble in overcrowded jails, and consequences of mandatory sentencing laws that prevent judges from judging.

Many of the new laws "can't be carried into effect with the resources that are in place," James Chaffe, president of the Canadian Association of Crown Counsels—the lawyers who prosecute people charged with crime—told the committee. The criminal justice system, he said, is "critically overburdened," and already unable to "consistently carry into effect many of our criminals laws." The new laws will "exacerbate what is already a dangerous situation," resulting in plea bargains, withdrawal of charges, and other troubles, according to Chaffe.

As for jail conditions, the "correctional system is headed for an acute double-bunking situation," with an expected 3,700 additional prisoners in 2014, Pierre Mallete, president of the Union of Canadian Correctional Officers, told the MPs. The result, he warned, will include increased risk of assault and suicide, and trouble identifying "who is making brew or moonshine or stocking drugs, weapons, and contraband."

Mandatory sentencing for just drug crimes will "create all manner of injustices," resulting in "the jailing of untold numbers of Canadians who do not deserve to be there," and cost taxpayers "billions of dollars," defence lawyer Kirk Tousaw wrote in a *Toronto Star* article October 31, 2011. Tousaw cited the case of Mrs. B., a 67-year-old grandmother of four who had obtained legal authority from a doctor to smoke marijuana in order to relieve acute chronic pain from arthritis and fibromyalgia, without the debilitating side effects she had suffered from pharmaceuticals. Mrs. B., however, had neglected to forward the doctor's papers to Ottawa for a required licence before she began puffing. She later obtained the licence, but not in time to avoid being charged and hauled into court. The judge hearing the case dismissed the charge. He could not have done that if the amended laws of the *Safe Streets and Communities Act* had been in effect. Grandma would have spent a year in jail, her life would have been ruined, and taxpayers would have been stuck with more than $100,000 in prison costs, because of a technicality.

Bundling amendments to so many laws (the *Act's* title mentions the criminal code, four specific Acts, "and other *Acts*") drew criticism. This is "not in the spirit of Canada's democratic process," complained the Canadian Bar Association, noting that several critical initiatives had not been reviewed by any Parliamentary committee, and amendments to other, earlier bills, previously agreed to by Parliamentary committees, had been dropped.

Overcrowded jails will bring greater risk of assault and suicide, and trouble identifying "who is making brew or stocking drugs, weapons, and contraband."

One result of bundling is that major supporters endorsed only "most" of the Bill, while opponents found sections they liked. The Canadian Bar Association, for example, faulted the Bill as a "punitive approach" to criminal law that neglected "prevention and rehabilitation... most likely to contribute to public safety," while replicating policies that elsewhere failed "at enormous public expense." Yet the CBA supported amendments to the *Justice for Victims of Terrorism* law contained in the Act. An all or nothing Bill prevents members of Parliament from voting for the what they deem to be the best and opposing the worst.

The highest profile item in the bundle of new laws is the changes to the *Youth Criminal Justice* law. The government first introduced a bill to change this law in November 2007, igniting four years of controversy. The changes sought then and achieved now are said by the government to be a response to the Nunn report, a 386-public inquiry report by retired Nova Scotia Supreme Court Justice Merlin Nunn, on a case that clearly highlighted the need for change in the youth law.

When 16-year-old boy (identified as AB in Nunn's report, but referred to as "Archie Bunker" in news reports) faced 38 criminal charges in a Halifax court, mostly related to car thefts and drug charges, he was released on bail. The judge had no option, because that is what the youth law required.

Two days later, Bunker, high on drugs, led police on a 20-minute chase at 180 km-h, before crashing into a car driven by Theresa McEvoy, a 52-year-old teacher and mother of two, killing her. Bunker was released from jail after serving 36 months of a 54-month sentence, despite a finding by the National Parole Board that he had not been rehabilitated, had continued to behave badly in jail, and maintained "criminally ingrained values." He was released because that is what the youth law required.

In his report on the Bunker case, Judge Nunn called not only for changes in the youth law to prevent the release of dangerous young criminals, but also greater focus on preventing youth crime and violence. "We can move ahead to a greater level of success in preventing youth crime," Nunn wrote.

The government's 2007 bill to amend the youth law was an issue in the 2008 national elections. Opposition politicians accused the government of an agenda to lock up more youth than just those considered dangerously violent. "Demagoguery based on fear, not reason," said Liberal Leader Stephane Dion. "Prison is a university of crime for a 14-year-old," said Bloc Quebecois Leader Gilles Duceppe. Judge Nunn was equally critical of the Bill said to be a response to his report. "Custody should be the last ditch thing for a child," he told *Canadian Press*. If you "lock the door and put away the key," then "instead of reha-bilitating him, you've got a kid that may be 10 times worse than when he went in."

The arguments inevitably rose again in the Parliamentary hearings in the final months of 2011. Perhaps the strongest voice came from an organization with just eight members, the child and youth advocates appointed by the legislatures or governments of all provinces except Prince Edward Island and New Brunswick. The four governments that supported the omnibus legislation clearly did not speak for their child and youth advocates.

"We see no evidence that shows that the proposed amendments to the [youth] *Act* will decrease youth crime or that they will increase the safety of the Canadian public," Mary Ellen Tupel-Lafond, chair of the Canadian Council of Child and Youth Advocates, told the MPs. "We must not respond by locking up more youth and handing out more adult sentences to youth," which she said has typically "worse outcomes for children and youth," while increasing the chances for more youth crime.

It will take years to gauge the effect of the new laws. If the government and its supporters are correct, billions of dollars will make Canadian streets and communities safer. If the critics are correct, the justice system and jails may breakdown from overload, crime will increase, Canadians may be less safe, and billions of dollars will have been wasted. Time will tell.

Character assassination

Critics of the Harper government have been subjected to character assassination, intimidation, and firings. Diplomat Richard Colvin and veterans' advocate Sean Bruyea are the two who have been most prominently subject to intimidation, abusive in Colvin's case and also illegal in Bruyea's.

Colvin, Canada's second ranking diplomat in the Afghanistan war in 2006, claimed that Canada was complicit in the torture, and possibly execution, by Afghanistan authorities of Afghanistan prisoners, or detainees, turned over to Afghanistan authorities for questioning. If true, Canada may have been in violation of international law.

Colvin sent 17 written reports (they have never been made public) to senior military and government authorities warning about torture by the Afghanistan authorities. He was told to shut up. He told a Parliamentary committee that he had received "written messages from the senior Canadian government coordinator for Afghanistan to the effect that I should be quiet and do what I was told, and also phone messages from a DFAIT [Department of Foreign Affairs and International Trade] assistant deputy minister suggesting that in future, we should not put things on paper, but instead use the telephone."

"We detained and handed over for severe torture, a lot of innocent people... truck drivers, tailors, peasants."

Colvin did not keep quiet. "We detained and handed over for severe torture, a lot of innocent people... truck drivers, tailors, peasants," Colvin told the Parliamentary committee investigating the issue. "Instead of winning hearts and minds, we caused Kandaharis to fear foreigners. Canada's detainee practices alienated us from the population and strengthened the insurgency," Colvin said.

Colvin's allegations were given added weight by an unedited copy of a government document leaked to the *Globe and Mail.* "Extrajudicial executions, disappearances, torture and detention without trial are all too common," the government report stated.

The government refused to provide documents about the issue requested by the Parliamentary committee. Rather than risking a contempt of Parliament vote that could bring the government down, Stephen Harper persuaded Governor General Michaelle Jean to sign a proclamation shutting down Parliament for a three-month "recess."

While all this was going on, Amnesty International and the B.C. Civil Liberties Association filed an application in the Federal Court for an order to stop the prisoner transfer: a case that could well have determined whether Canada was guilty or innocent of complicity in the torture and perhaps execution of prisoners. The case was never heard. The government argued, and the courts agreed, that the Charter of Rights and Freedoms on which the court application was based, did not apply to actions of Canadian soldiers outside of Canada. Calls for a public inquiry have gone unheeded. The issue is probably dead.

For proclaiming the truth as he saw it, Colvin was attacked with innuendoes that questioned his competency, integrity and loyalty, and suggestions that he was a Taliban sympathizer, or soft on terrorism. In the House of Commons, Defence Minister Peter MacKay described Colvin as a "suspect source," who had been duped by Taliban lies. More than 100 former Canadian ambassadors signed a public letter, protesting that Colvin had been "unfairly subjected to personal attacks" and "aspersions cast on his personal integrity."

"The Colvin affair risks creating a climate in which [Foreign Service] Officers may be more inclined to report what they believe headquarters wants to hear, rather than facts and perceptions deemed unpalatable," the former ambassadors wrote.

Medical records disclosed

Private medical information was illegally disclosed and widely distributed by the Harper government in its efforts to discredit and intimidate veterans' advocate Sean Bruyea. The confidential medical files were distributed by the Department of Veterans Affairs to cabinet members and their political staffs, who spread it to hundreds of others. Bruyea, a retired Air Force intelligence officer and a veteran of the 1991 Gulf war, is a leading advocate for improved treatment of wounded veterans and their families, and a sharp critic of the Conservative government. The release of medical records stressed the life of Bruyea and his wife for a period of five years.

Privacy Commission Jennifer Stoddart, as early as 2006, advised Veteran Affairs Minister Greg Thompson that a departmental briefing note about Bruyea contained "considerable sensitive medical information, including diagnosis, symptoms, chronology of interactions with the department as a client, amount of financial benefits received, frequency of appointments and recommended treatment paths."

Three years later (October 7, 2010), Stoddart ruled that the release of the documents was an "alarming" violation of the *Privacy Act.* "The veteran's sensitive medical and personal information was shared— seemingly with no controls—among departmental officials who had no legitimate need to see them," Stoddart wrote.

Nineteen months earlier, Bruyea had filed a $400,000 lawsuit against Attorney General Rob Nicholson and three bureaucrats, claiming the documents were used to "falsely portray me and my advocacy to help other veterans as merely a manifestation of an unstable mind." The lawsuit was settled out of court six weeks after Stoddart's ruling.

The government is also alleged to have violated the personal files of former veterans ombudsman Pat Stogran and other veterans.

Afterword

Canada will endure. No matter how tried, twisted and tortured by misfortune, mismanagement and malice; political lies, confusion and corruption; the wages of greed; and malevolent forces of nature, Canada will endure.

We can see that more clearly in an Afterword than we could in a Foreword. When we look back to see how it is that we got to where we are, we can look forward, if not with clarity at least with confidence.

We can see the looming clouds of a gathering storm but we can look forward with confidence because of who we are as a people and a society.

We are a society of conservative prudence and liberal values.

Our prudence is reflected in our founding Constitution, with its proclamation of "Peace, order, and good government." We may not have always attained those ideals, but we have come as close as anyone.

Our Canadian values are universal values, as befits the world's most universal people. We are the leading proponent of universal values. We are the nation that authored the United Nation's *Universal Declaration of Human Rights,* the shining model of universal values, no matter how imperfect the United Nations or the world in attaining those values.

We are a people shaped by our diversity, by our history, and by our vast, northern, rugged and sometimes harsh geography. We sweat in the heat of blazing hot summers and shiver in winter Arctic winds. We smell the delicate fragrance of the wild rose, hear the call of the loon and the cry of the whippoorwill, if only on rare escapes from our teeming cities. We cope.

We escaped largely unscathed the years of economic hardship, loss and suffering that fell on the United States and Europe in 2008. We escaped because of good governance, and, in large measure, because of the economic boon of the Alberta oil sands.

We escaped because good governance and sound financial regulation avoided the housing bubble and malfeasance of virtually unregulated big banks and giant investment firms, which triggered the financial and economic collapse.

But in almost single-minded economic reliance on oil production we have forgotten that ever since Canada gave birth to the petroleum industry in 1858 this had been an industry with a notorious cycle of glut and shortage, boom and bust. When Canada emerged from the Second World War, our reliance on imported oil for more than 90 percent of our petroleum needs was an economic drag. Alberta was one of the poorest provinces. Then came the discovery of Alberta's big oil fields and what author Eric Hanson in 1958 dubbed *The Dynamic Decade,* as wealth poured into Alberta.

We soon found that no one wanted our oil, and that it would be less costly to buy it from the Arabs than produce it ourselves. The United States imposed tight limits on the amount of our oil that American firms were allowed to import. Our own needs could have been more cheaply supplied from the vastly greater resources of the Persian Gulf where oil could be produced almost as abundantly and cheaply as water.

Alberta's oil industry was rescued by Ontario. Throughout the 1960s, the National Oil Policy banned from Ottawa west the use of low-cost imported crude oil and refined petroleum products. That imposed a price premium of half a billion dollars, paid largely by Ontario consumers. It was a consumer-paid subsidy that sustained Alberta's oil industry in a time of need. That is something we have forgotten, but timely to recall.

The latest oil glut is growing, and could be the most profound in the petroleum industry's 154 years of history. Iraq alone is expected to soon add some seven million barrels a day to the world's available oil supply. That supply addition might be greatly exceeded by technology that fractures shale rocks to yield both natural gas and crude oil. "Fracing" has profoundly revolutionized the North American supply of natural gas, the fossil fuel that admits the least amount of greenhouse gas emissions. Now it's profoundly revolutionizing the oil supply, with some predicting that the United States will be transformed from the world's largest oil importer to petroleum self-sufficiency. And the potential isn't limited to North America. Every continent has shale that can be released by fracing, potentially in quantities that could double world oil production capacity.

While developing and potential oil and natural gas supplies increase, demand will be throttled back by global warming, the darkest cloud that shadows the twenty-first century. Burning less greenhouse-gas-emitting fossil fuels is the only assured way to curb the already increasing frequency and intensity of death and destruction caused by global-warming-induced hurricanes, tornadoes, wildfires, drought, floods, rising ocean levels, and other ill effects.

We confront the confluence of this storm with so much of our economy nestled in the oil sands basket. There has been no serious effort to reduce energy consumption, no fallback, no plan B, no effort to support development of clean, green fuels that reduce the world's greenhouse gas emissions. We continue to rely on the fuels of yesterday to meet the needs of today and tomorrow.

It is not too late. If the storm seems overwhelming, that, too, is because we ignore our history. We have overcome every storm to build the best country in the world. We will continue to do so, with the same pain and perseverance.

Canada will endure.

Index

Printed by Publishers Graphics Canada Inc